Praise for *Wait, How Do I Write This Email?*

"Danny Rubin's no-nonsense guide to effective writing is sure to make anyone a better communicator. If you've ever wondered, 'How should I phrase that?', this is your go-to source."

— JENNA GOUDREAU, DEPUTY EDITOR OF BUSINESS INSIDER

"Take one look at the table of contents, and you'll understand how much these templates could boost your career and help you build relationships. Read Danny's book—you're going to need it."

— DAN SCHAWBEL, BESTSELLING AUTHOR OF
PROMOTE YOURSELF AND *ME 2.0*

"*Wait, How Do I Write This Email?* gives the average job seeker a fighting chance in today's job search landscape. Danny addresses some of the most intimidating aspects of a person's career and provides simple how-to guides for the reader to put into practice."

— CASIDY LEMONS, TALENT ACQUISITION AT
GENERAL MOTORS COMPANY

"There are some books you keep by your desk, others you keep by your nightstand and a few you take on vacation. *Wait, How Do I Write This Email?* qualifies as all three and will make you better from the minute you open it."

— JONATHAN JACKSON, PROGRAM MANAGER FOR
CONSUMER CONTENT AT LINKEDIN

"Millennials are passionate about finding the career path that makes them happy. With each email template, Danny helps you take action steps to build the career you want and attain a work/life balance. Great resource!"

— CHELSEA KROST, MILLENNIAL EXPERT AND CO-FOUNDER
OF THE MPULSE, A DIGITAL MARKETING AGENCY

"Wow! What Danny Rubin has created should be THE required career manual for every college graduate, young professional, savvy professional, and basically anyone who communicates. In any fashion. Danny Rubin is the guru of 21st century communication. This book is bursting with so much practical and actionable wisdom that following just one of Danny's deep insights will not only pay for the price of the book, it might just save your career."

— PAUL ANGONE, AUTHOR OF *101 SECRETS FOR YOUR TWENTIES* AND
ALL GROAN UP: SEARCHING FOR SELF, FAITH, AND A FREAKING JOB!

"Most job seekers do not have the training or resources to know how to formulate a concise, impactful email to an employer to help them land a job. Danny's book will guide job seekers in writing the most appropriate email to that employer."

— SHIRA ITZHAK, OWNER OF REMEDY INTELLIGENT STAFFING

"The most recurring complaint academics hear from employers focuses squarely on poor writing skills of young professionals. Danny's book will become an important resource for corporations and universities seeking to improve written communications of employees and students."

— RON CULP, PROFESSIONAL DIRECTOR OF THE GRADUATE PUBLIC RELATIONS &
ADVERTISING PROGRAM AT DEPAUL UNIVERSITY

"Danny's book is a perfect resource for workforce development centers and youth service providers across the country. There are so many people who are unemployed or underemployed who would rely on a guide that teaches effective writing skills in the job market."

— LISA WORNOM-ZAHRALDDIN, MS, CWDP, PROGRAM MANAGER FOR THE
NATIONAL ASSOCIATION OF WORKFORCE DEVELOPMENT PROFESSIONALS

"*Wait, How Do I Write This Email?* is your new career glossary. You will find any template or quick idea to connect your career aspirations to a real person in a real, effective way. Don't wait. Use it now!"

— JON MERTZ, AUTHOR AND FOUNDER OF THIN DIFFERENCE

"Danny's focus on practical writing skills is a much-needed complement to the work we do helping young people align their passion with purpose in the job market."

— ADAM SMILEY POSWOLSKY, AUTHOR OF *THE QUARTER-LIFE BREAKTHROUGH*

Wait, How Do I Write This Email?

Game-Changing Templates
for Networking
and the Job Search

Danny Rubin

For information about this title or to order books and/or electronic
media, contact the publisher at www.newstoliveby.net.

Library of Congress Control Number: 2015906817

ISBN: 978-0-9963499-0-1 (Print)
978-0-9963499-1-8 (Ebook)

Printed in the United States of America

Cover design: Paul McCarthy

Interior design: 1106 Design

Publisher's Cataloging-In-Publication Data

TO ANYONE WITH A GREAT STORY TO TELL.
THAT MEANS YOU.

CONTENTS

Introduction

Hi there. I'm Danny Rubin.

I realize we met a minute ago, but I can already tell you have big plans for your career and intend to make an impact. I mean, a *real* impact. The kind where your talent, passion and ambition collide in a beautiful explosion to better the lives of everyone around you.

How do I know?

Well, you picked up this book. That means you recognize writing skills are a critical aspect of career development and business success. Plenty of people dream big dreams, but only a select few can put their vision into words and move others to action.

With *Wait, How Do I Write This Email?*, I help you turn routine situations into game-changing opportunities.

A networking email isn't a burden; it's your chance to make a lasting impression before you ever shake hands.

A job search email isn't a chore; it's a way to demonstrate poise and confidence.

And a cover letter isn't an imposition; it's how to tell your story and stand out from the competition.

Wait, How Do I Write This Email? is a teaching tool and reference guide. As you compose professional documents and emails, refer to my chapters on brevity and etiquette to stay sharp. When you need to write/revise your resume or compose job application emails, you can use my 100+ templates to structure the message and hit "Send" with confidence.

As you read this book, keep in mind great leaders are more than effective organizers, managers and public speakers. They are people who understand the power of the written word in our noisy digital age.

Strong writing is a remarkable tool, and I'm excited to show you why. I encourage you to read the opening chapters on writing skills before you use the templates. That way, you will understand the fundamentals and be ready to compose effective emails and documents.

Now let's get started.

We have important work to do.

Author's Notes

Before you begin, two points about the book:

1. I use the writing lessons and templates in the book when I lead communications workshops for college students, recent graduates and young professionals.

    I often see the guides help millennials open doors, begin conversations and move ahead in their careers. Still, it's important to keep in mind the book doesn't guarantee new relationships, job interviews, job offers or acceptance to graduate schools. The best we can do is work hard to make each message a memorable one.

2. All the people, schools, businesses and organizations I name in the guides and templates are fictitious.

Chapter 1

How to Write Everything Better

How to be Brief

YOU MAY NOT REALIZE IT, BUT YOU'RE A PROFESSIONAL WRITER.

Every day, you type words on the screen and place them before your friends, colleagues, clients and extended network. In essence, you put your writing ability on display for everyone to see.

That's why in Chapter 1, I show you easy ways to edit your work and improve how it looks and feels to the reader. Use these resources as you send emails, write job applications and correspond with people online.

In order to learn extremely effective writing skills, it's quite important that you are paying close attention and following instructions.

By the end of this chapter, you'll recognize all the problems with the above sentence. I count five issues. (Find an improved version on page 17.)

OK. Let's dive in.

THE ONE QUESTION EVERY GREAT COMMUNICATOR ASKS

"Do I need it?"

Everything you write, whether an email to one person or a presentation to 5,000 people, requires the "Do I need it?" treatment. When you cut what you don't need, your argument becomes stronger and more discernible. Two key parts of the deletion process:

- Remove extraneous words that make your writing too long (more on page 3)
- Remove ideas and arguments that distract the reader (more on page 6)

Questions to ask as you work on professional documents:

Resumes

- Do you provide too many bullet points under each job? Three is usually a good benchmark, although you may only have room for one or two (more info on page 215).
- Are you too wordy as you describe your duties at each company? Less is more.
- Is some of the information so old it's no longer relevant? For example, you list every internship even though you've worked for five years. Time to hit delete.

Cover Letters

- Do you explain how the job will boost your own career? Instead, focus on how you can help the company prosper.
- Do you include unnecessary details about your life? Focus on what's relevant to the job.
- Does your cover letter summarize your resume? That's boring. Better to use the letter to tell one great story. More on the "storytelling" cover letter on page 195.

Speeches and Presentations

- Practice your speech in front of someone else. Ask the person, "Does it go on too long?" If yes, read through each section and then ask yourself, "Do I need it?" Either find sections to remove, or you'll give a dull speech.
- Does your talk occasionally drift from the main topic or central argument? Locate parts that aren't essential and remove them.

- Do you spend too much time on any one topic? Are there sections you can cut out entirely? If so, delete them.
- A speech isn't about you. It's about the people in the crowd who take your message to heart. "Does the *audience* need to hear it?" That's what counts.

Emails

- Does the reader have to hunt to find your main point? Help the person out.

   NOTE: What's essential? The main argument or one big request. Everything else deserves the "Do I need it?" treatment.

- Do you devote too many words to the problem? The reader would prefer you lay out a solution.
- Is the email you're about to send necessary at all?

We are trained to think the "delete" key is a negative. Like we only press the button when we screw up. Nonsense.

The "delete" key is the most important command on the keyboard. With every stroke, we strengthen our writing.

How to improve everything you write in three minutes

The tutorial below allows you to improve anything you write in a few short minutes. Keep these pages handy!

STEP ONE: When you finish your document, hit CTRL+F to bring up the search function.

STEP TWO: One by one, look for these words and delete/amend them.

- very, just and really (remove all three)
- that (delete, as in "I believe that you are correct")
- quite (delete, excess word)
- thing (replace with specific word for the "thing")
- utilize (switch to "use" or pick another verb)

- get or got (pick another, more descriptive verb)
- -ing verbs ("The boy is running" becomes "The boy runs")*

STEP THREE: Read over your work to check your edits.

*The "-ing" verbs bullet point deserves further explanation. At the start of an email, you may want to use the phrase "I am writing" as in "I am writing to introduce myself." In my view, that's an acceptable use of an "-ing" verb because it's the best way to begin. "I write to introduce myself" is too stilted.

In many other cases, you can cut the "-ing" and the sentence still makes sense. Here's one more example with multiple "-ing" words:

*At my most recent job, I was responsible for **managing** projects, **working** with clients and **overseeing** our budget.*

Let's chop down the three "-ing" verbs.

*At my most recent job, I **managed** projects, **worked** with clients and **oversaw** our budget.*

The original sentence has 18 words and 31 syllables.

The revised sentence has 15 words and 22 syllables.

Brevity makes you sharper. Plain and simple.

"Filler" words to cut out and why

Let's go a bit further than the "three minute" exercise. Here are five more words and phrases you need to delete, along with an explanation for why you shouldn't use them.

1. Amazing

In an unscientific poll I conducted by...well, observing the conversations around me, I have concluded "amazing" is the most overused word in our vocabulary.

Why? A word that means everything actually means nothing.

"Man, that show was so amazing last night. What an amazing crowd and the guitar solo at the end? Amazing."

See my point?

Words to use instead of "amazing": fascinating, astounding, breathtaking, spectacular, terrific, magnificent and unbelievable. Need more? Grab a thesaurus.

2. Definitely

Like "amazing," the word "definitely" has become a filler term. You can remove "definitely" and the sentence retains its meaning.

"I am definitely glad Susan was at the happy hour to help with the awkward conversation."

Becomes...

"I am glad Susan was at the happy hour to help with the awkward conversation."

Same difference.

Also, no more "definately." There's only one correct spelling.

3. Literally

"This is literally the funniest thing I've ever seen..."

"You have literally got to be kidding me..."

"Are you literally about to do this?"

"Literally" has also become a filler word, an uninspiring adverb with zero flavor or style.

Delete whenever possible. The word *literally* does nothing for you.

4. In Order

The words "in order" may turn up in our writing for three reasons:

▸ We try to make our sentences more professional.

▸ We use them out of habit.

▸ We assume the two words *need* to be there.

For example, "I wrote this line in order to show you how to use less words."

If we remove "in order," the meaning stays the same.

"I wrote this line to show you how to use less words."

5. Such As

A tiny phrase, sure, but "such as" screams out, "I'm trying to impress you!"

For example, "My internship taught me a range of skills **such as** project management, problem solving and time management."

People rarely use "such as" in normal conversation. So why write it?

Instead, use "like" as in "My internship taught me a range of skills **like** project coordination, problem solving and time management."

When you finish writing and start the revision process (hint: print out the page to spot errors), make sure you search the document for "such as."

Remember: when it comes to documents **like** job applications, the reader is the only one who matters.

How to remove big sections of text

Now that we have covered easy ways to remove words and short phrases, let's turn our attention to big ideas and chunks of words.

Cover letter, presentation, speech, formal work document — you should edit **EVERYTHING** you write. Before you consider a document "finalized," be tough on yourself and chop it down.

No one will ever say, "This person's document is way too **short**. Now what am I supposed to do with all my free time?"

I created a chart to help tighten your writing. Are the rules hard and fast? No. They are a reminder to give people exactly what they need and not a word more.

Length of Document	Number of Words to Remove
300 words	50–60
400 words	75–85
500 words	100–110
600 words	125–135
700 words	150–160
800 words	175–185
900 words	200–210
1,000 words	225–235
1,000+ words	At least 250

Questions to Ask as You Remove Words

- ▸ Is each sentence — or part of the sentence — absolutely necessary to make your point?
- ▸ Do any sentences repeat a point already made?
- ▸ Which sections are **least** essential?
- ▸ If you HAD to remove a paragraph, which one would it be?
- ▸ Does it "feel" like a section drags or slows down the pace?

#1 Rule: Never fall in love with a particular line.

Let's look at three examples to understand how we delete chunks of words.

1. Two paragraphs of a personal statement for graduate school

"Too long" version:

> My career path so far has been unconventional but valuable every step of the way. Yes, I could have gone the usual route like my peers: graduate college, dive into a regular 9-to-5 job, wear a suit and tie and battle every day in traffic, but that life doesn't appeal to me. It might be a great option for others, but I had different plans. After graduation, I decided to go down a road few people would consider, and it's made all the difference in my life. I joined a service organization and spent two years in a village in Madagascar.
>
> When I arrived in the village, I wanted to turn around and run home. I felt so alone and out of my comfort zone. Sure, in college I had traveled a good amount. I studied abroad in Barcelona, which is where I learned to speak Spanish fluently. But now I was in Africa and my Spanish skills wouldn't be much use. With the help of a local fisherman named Haja, I integrated into the culture of the village and...

OK, that's enough. As you read those two paragraphs, did you notice how they wander and lose focus? The writer repeats the same ideas and includes information that distracts from the main point: why the experience in a service organization makes the person an ideal fit for the graduate program.

Key sections to delete:

> Yes, I could have gone the usual route like my peers: graduate college, dive into a regular 9-to-5 job, wear a suit and tie and battle every day in traffic, but that life doesn't appeal to me. It might be a great option for others, but I had different plans.

Wonderful for you but not essential information. Delete.

> Sure, in college I had traveled a good amount. I studied abroad in Barcelona, which is where I learned to speak Spanish fluently. But now I was in Africa and my Spanish skills wouldn't be much use.

Not necessary to include. Delete.

The "much shorter" version:

> After graduation, I decided to go down a road few others would consider, and it's made all the difference in my life. I joined a service organization and spent two years in a village in Madagascar.

> When I arrived in the village, I wanted to turn around and run home. With the help of a local fisherman named Haja, I integrated into the culture of the village and…

Faster, sharper, more focused. In the second version, the writer eliminates information that's redundant or unnecessary. Ask yourself:

- ▸ Do I stray from the main point?
- ▸ Do I provide extraneous information?

Be tough on yourself. Be critical.

2. One paragraph of a big email to coworkers

"Too long" version:

> I want to address what happened last night at the gala, why the evening became chaotic and how our team needs to improve to make sure what happened never happens again. I have received numerous complaints either in person or over email from people who were upset with the food, our service and how we mixed up entrees for over 50 people. In all my years of event planning, I have never been so embarrassed by a team's performance, and again I hope this email can help us improve, especially because we have another big dinner on Saturday night, and we need to be at our best. Now, the first problem we need to correct is communication between the kitchen and the servers. It's a simple process: talk with the chefs before dinner service begins and make sure they understand how many meals to cook that are fish, chicken or vegetarian. That's a basic, fundamental part of the night for us. All you need to do is keep an open dialogue, and we won't have these food screw-ups. The second issue is...

Whew. Are you exhausted from that paragraph? I am. And I wrote it!

Can you pick out the sentences with redundant information? Did you choose these three?

> I want to address what happened last night at the gala, why the evening became chaotic and how our team needs to improve to make sure what happened never happens again.

> I have never been so embarrassed by a team's performance, and again I hope this email can help us improve, especially because we have another big dinner on Saturday night, and we need to be at our best.

> All you need to do is keep an open dialogue, and we won't have these food screw-ups.

We can delete parts of each sentence or the entire section because all three are repetitive.

Also, the paragraph itself is way too long. Let the reader take in each sentence and give the message room to breathe.

The "much shorter" version:

> I want to address what happened last night at the gala and how our team needs to improve. I have received numerous complaints either in person or over email from people who were upset with the food, our service and how we mixed up entrees for over 50 people.

> We have another big dinner on Saturday night, and we need to be at our best.

> Now, the first problem we need to correct is communication between the kitchen and the servers. It's a simple process: talk with the chefs before dinner service begins and make sure they understand how many meals to cook that are fish, chicken or vegetarian.

> The second issue is…

Not only does the revised version read better, but it also makes the person more authoritative. Less words = more impact. And I like this sentence as its own line:

> We have another big dinner on Saturday night, and we need to be at our best.

Now the sentence has "umph" and power. It's not buried inside a huge paragraph.

One more key strategy: when you make a point, don't dwell on it. People understand you the first time.

3. Intro paragraph of an important speech to your team

Thank you, Sarah, for the kind introduction. And thank you for your hard work all year on some of our biggest client accounts. Today, I want to talk with everyone about where our company has gone and where I believe we are headed. You know, all year we work so hard and stay so focused on the bottom line, and we rarely have a chance to step back and assess our progress. Today, that's exactly what we're going to do. I promise to keep my remarks short so stay with me.

Everyone, next year we will need to make the biggest decision in the ten-year history of our company...

The intro paragraph is, in a word, terrible. The speaker immediately loses everyone's attention with empty rhetoric like:

You know, all year we work so hard and stay so focused on the bottom line, and we rarely have a chance to step back and assess our progress. Today, that's exactly what we're going to do.

And people in the audience sit there and think, "OK, start assessing already!"

In our third and final editing example, I will do the unthinkable. Yes, I will now delete an entire paragraph. Dun Dun Dunnnnnn.

The best writers know any sentence or paragraph is on the chopping block.

The "much shorter" version:

Thank you, Sarah, for the kind introduction.

(short pause)

Everyone, next year we will need to make the biggest decision in the ten-year history of our company...

Boom. Now, the speech opens with some sizzle and drama. Skip the politically correct, uninspiring jargon. Get right to the good stuff. The audience is dialed in and ready to absorb the message.

Now, your turn. Look at your document, add up the words and find parts to remove. Also, you might want to approach people you respect to review your work.

Ask them, "What parts are least essential? What can go?"

Then, let the deletions commence.

Why you shouldn't use adverbs

I used to be a fan of adverbs, in particular "ly" words. I would add them all the time for emphasis, as if the adjective alone wouldn't cut it.

Then I had a change of heart. In most cases, I realized adverbs are useless and take up space.

Like the kid at prom who reeks of cologne, adverbs try too hard to impress.

Resumes, cover letters, emails..."ly" words are everywhere. And today, it's time to say goodbye.

So long, adverb

Adverbs are fancy words that try to modify a phrase or sentence. They don't.

If you remove the adverb, the thought doesn't lose its meaning. Plus, your work reads faster. **Less is more.**

Watch what happens when these common "ly" adverbs go away.

– ~~Diligently~~ monitored all aspects of the project...

– ~~Fully~~ capable of working on the assignment...

– ~~Incredibly~~ excited to be here...

– ~~Particularly~~ interested in...

– ~~Positively~~ improved the office culture...

– ~~Completely~~ finished all work on time...

– ~~Reliably~~ consistent with all deadlines...

– ~~Sincerely~~ appreciated...

12

– ~~Uniquely~~ skilled at database management…

– ~~Unquestionably~~ the best team…

If you're "capable of working on the assignment," then "fully" is implied. DELETE. If you "finish" something, then of course you did "completely." Redundant. DELETE.

The next time you review your work, hit CTRL+F for "ly" words and let 'em go.

Quit the fancy talk

When you write above your comfort level, you appear as though you try too hard.

The secret? Write an employer like you would a friend. Be normal and conversational.

In short: **be yourself.**

Be Yourself in Email

Trying too hard: I wish to inquire about the possibility of your company expanding in the near future.

Simple translation: I'm curious to know if your company is hiring.

Trying too hard: My experience thus far has proven I have a distinguished track record and a penchant for success.

Simple translation: I have a proven track record in our field and here's why.

Note: Then you give concrete, detailed examples to back up the claim. That's how you make a job application valuable.

Trying too hard: If you are able to set aside time in your schedule, might we be able to meet for a face-to-face conversation, perhaps over coffee?

Simple translation: Are you free this week for coffee?

Trying too hard: My most recent job taught me the immense importance of human communication and why it's incumbent as an individual to stay in touch with my superiors on all work-related projects.

Simple translation: I know the importance of constant communication with all team members.

Note: Never refer to yourself as an "individual." That doesn't sound sophisticated. It sounds like you're part of some medical research project.

Trying too hard: The work I undertook in my previous position was arduous yet gratifying.

Simple translation: My most recent job was a challenge, but I came away with terrific experience. For example...

Trying too hard: I want to send along a short email and see if you have received my job application. When you have a moment, please let me know the status of my application.

Simple translation: Please let me know if you received my job application.

Be Yourself in a Resume or Cover Letter

Trying too hard: Assisted in the preparation and dissemination of all corporate social media communication with internal staff and outside clientele.

Simple translation: Created content for the company's various social media channels.

Trying too hard: Served as executive assistant to the program's executive director, handled a variety of critical inter-office assignments and liaised with senior staffers on major national accounts.

Simple translation: As executive assistant, I drafted office-wide memorandums, conducted research for senior staffers and made sure the executive director never missed a meeting despite a non-stop schedule.

*Note: Don't be fancy and vague. Tell us **exactly** what you did. And never use "liaised." Yuck.*

14

Bring all the lessons together

To conclude, here is a sample email with examples of all the writing lessons we covered. In the sample, you will find:

- ▶ The "Do I need it?" rule
- ▶ Common words we can always delete
- ▶ "Filler" words we need to replace
- ▶ Big sections of text we can do without
- ▶ Useless adverbs
- ▶ Fancy talk turned simple

Scenario: A job search email to a friend so he can forward your info to an employer

Hi Allen,

Thanks for the help with the job search. I am hoping you can pass along my information in order to let your company CFO know I'm interested in the sales position.

Right away, we have several "red flags."

- ▶ *"I am hoping" is a drawn out way to write "I hope." Remember to remove "-ing" words.*

- ▶ *"in order" — The sentence remains the same if we remove "in order" and write "pass along my information to let your company CFO know I'm interested in the sales position."*

Next section:

I have worked extremely hard at my previous sales job at Acme Corporation and believe I am absolutely ready for the next opportunity. At the last job, I diligently handled external client relations and ensured every account received the necessary considerations when it comes to new products, service and training.

OK, even more issues.

- ▶ *"extremely," "absolutely" and "diligently" — we can delete all three adverbs*

15

▸ *"ensured every account received the necessary considerations when it comes to new products, service and training." — a lot of fancy talk here; how about "made sure every account received the necessary products, service and training."?*

Next section:

I'm not sure how well you know the CFO, but I'm curious if he has a timeline for the open position. I'd also like to know the kind of sales associate he wants to hire. I see the position asks for someone with four years of experience, and while I only have two I still think I am qualified for the job.

The above paragraph fits two of my "need to delete" criteria: a big chunk of text and the "Do I need it?" question. If you send along information an employer might see, why dwell on the negative?

Remove the entire sentence: "I see the position asks for someone with four years of experience, and while I only have two I still think I am qualified for the job."

The line will distract the reader and also put you in an unfavorable light. Delete.

Next section:

I have attached my resume to the email. Again, I am looking forward to hearing what the CFO thinks.

Thanks,

– Dave Matson

Finally, we find more excess words and phrases.

▸ *"looking forward to hearing" changes to "I look forward to feedback from the CFO" — no more "-ing" verbs*

From the top, the corrected email reads:

Hi Allen,

Thanks for the help with the job search. I hope you can pass along my information to let your company CFO know I'm interested in the sales position.

I have worked hard at my previous sales job at Acme Corporation and believe I am ready for the next opportunity. At my last job, I handled external client relations and made sure every account received the necessary products, service and training.

I'm not sure how well you know the CFO, but I'm curious if he has a timeline for the open position. I'd also like to know the kind of sales associate he wants to hire.

I have attached my resume to the email. Again, I look forward to feedback from the CFO.

Thanks,

– Dave Matson

Answer key: incorrect sentence from the chapter introduction

Original sentence:

In order to learn **extremely** effective writing skills, it's **quite** important **that** you are **paying** close attention and **following** instructions.

The five mistakes:

1. Remove "in order" (excess)
2. Remove "extremely" (unnecessary adverb)
3. Remove "quite" (excess)
4. Remove "that" (excess)
5. Remove "- ing" from "paying" and "following"

Corrected version:

To learn effective writing skills, you must pay close attention and follow instructions.

The best way to do a final edit

After you've done spot edits (ex: hit CTRL+F and search for extra words like "in order" and "that"), how do you tackle one last read-through?

The key is to peel ourselves from the screen (phone, tablet, laptop or desktop). We stare at a document or email for so long we lose the ability to catch mistakes. We need a fresh perspective, and the best method is to give our eyes a rest.

To that end, here's my recommendation (see next page).

How to Edit
by Danny Rubin

1. Print out the document.

2. Leave your desk and review the document somewhere else in the room or another room entirely.

3. Read the document aloud to see if any sentences have missing words, the wrong words, misspelled words or seem awkward when spoken.

4. Make your edits with a pen.

5. Return to your desk and make the edits on the screen.

6. Congrats! You edited the document like a pro.

For more editing tips, visit newstoliveby.net

How to be interesting

IN THE LAST SECTION, I EXPLAINED THE POWER OF BREVITY AND WHY LESS IS MORE. STILL, IF YOU CUT A DOCUMENT FROM 500 WORDS TO 350, HOW CAN YOU MAKE THE REMAINING 350 STAND OUT?

The topics I address in this chapter will teach you how to turn vague, nondescript language into engaging copy.

Let me put it another way. In "How to be Brief," we trimmed the fat. Now, we season the meat and grill to perfection.

Got it? I don't want you to think, "Danny told me to be brief, and now he wants me to ADD words? What's the deal here?"

The best writers edit when they must and include when they must.

By the end of this section, you will understand what I mean.

QUANTIFY QUANTIFY QUANTIFY

Did you know strong communicators also excel at math? I don't mean algebra and trigonometry but rather the ability to use numbers to strengthen a piece of writing.

Here's an example in a cover letter:

> "Every day I would make the long commute from my apartment out into rural Oklahoma to work at the school."

Long commute? **How** long? Let's quantify the sentence.

> "Every day I would make the 90-minute commute from my apartment out into rural Oklahoma to work at the school."

Ninety minutes. **That's** how long. The number (90) makes the sentence more precise and your journey more interesting.

Let's quantify again, this time on a resume:

> "Accomplished and dedicated sales representative with a track record of success."

> Here, there's no easy way to add a number (like when we changed "long commute" to "90-minute commute").

> To quantify the resume example, we need to reconstruct the sentence. First, ask key questions.

> Accomplished sales representative? **How** accomplished?

> Track record of success? **How** successful?

> "Dedicated sales representative who in 2014 generated $2.1 million in profit and grew client base from 18 to 27."

Do you see the power of numbers? As you write, read each sentence closely and look for opportunities to quantify (ex: statistics, hard data and dollar figures).

Numbers make your point and help you stand out.

Never be vague!

Always go one layer deeper

The most vivid writing has multiple layers. With every new detail, a sentence becomes more colorful and memorable.

Here's a line you might find in a cover letter:

"After college, I taught English at a school in China."

OK, cool experience. But look what happens when I add one layer.

"After college, I taught English at a school in *rural* China."

Now we picture the person in a remote location. Before I added "rural," we pictured...well, nothing. We imagined a person who taught somewhere on a map in China.

Let's add another layer:

"After college, I taught English *speaking skills* at a school in rural China."

Again, the story becomes more appealing. Now we envision the person teaching a class of people to speak the English language.

Another layer:

"After college, I taught English speaking skills *to a group of 25 school-age boys* at a school in rural China."

The plot thickens again. The person taught children to speak English — and a lot of them.

Another layer:

"After college, I taught English speaking skills *for one year* to a group of 25 school-age boys at a school in rural China.

And one final time:

"After college, I taught English speaking skills for one year to a group of 25 school-age boys at a school in rural China, *more than 1,000 miles from the nearest major city.*"

Wow. That IS remote.

The sentence at the beginning:

"After college, I taught English at a school in China."

The sentence now:

"After college, I taught English speaking skills for one year to a group of 25 school-age boys at a school in rural China, more than 1,000 miles from the nearest major city."

Which sentence is more interesting? Obviously the second one.

As I explained in the intro to this section, brevity matters but not at the expense of telling your story in full.

To add layers, ask yourself WHO, WHAT, WHEN, WHERE, WHY and HOW.

21

"After college, I taught English at a school in China."

WHO did you teach? A group of 25 school-age boys

WHAT did you teach? English speaking skills

WHERE did you teach? Rural China, more than 1,000 miles from the nearest major city

HOW LONG did you teach? For one year

Quiz yourself like a news reporter and explore the sentence from all relevant angles.

More layers = more memorable.

The power of a wrinkle

Thank-you notes after a wedding teach us a lot about smart writing in the business world. Wedding thank-you notes come in two varieties:

1. Cookie-cutter
2. One of a kind

Everyone understands the difference between a generic TY note and a meaningful one. It's called a "wrinkle," a personal twist on a predictable approach.

1. Cookie-cutter TY note after the wedding

Hi Steve and Jenny,

Thank you so much for attending our wedding and for the generous gift. We can't imagine our wedding weekend without you and are so blessed to have such great friends in our lives. We hope to see you both really soon!

– Matt and Sharon

Clearly, Matt and Sharon wrote pretty much the same card to everyone who attended the wedding. A TY note is a nice gesture but only if the card has a special touch. In other words, a wrinkle.

2. One-of-a-kind TY note after a wedding

Hi Steve and Jenny,

Thank you so much for attending our wedding and for the set of wine glasses. Matt's 93-year-old grandmother, Rose, who couldn't make it to the wedding for travel reasons, came to our house last week and offered a toast with your wine glasses! It was a special moment, and you two made it happen. We are so blessed to have great friends like you in our lives, and we hope to see you both really soon!

– Matt and Sharon

Did you spot the wrinkle? Yep, the anecdote about the toast with the grandmother. The one-of-a-kind TY note is fridge-worthy and makes Jenny and Steve feel great. The cookie-cooker version? Headed straight for the trash.

The "wrinkle" method works in the business world too. Throughout the book, you will see I include a wrinkle in many of the email templates. Rather than jump right into business, I show you how to be conversational and interested in the other person. It's an approach to strengthen relationships, develop rapport and prove you're, well, one of a kind.

Here's an example from Chapter 3: Networking Templates

Page 65: How to write someone from a networking event about a job.

Hi _____,

It was great to meet you [earlier today/yesterday] at the [name of networking event]. I enjoyed our conversation about [reference a specific part of your discussion; for instance, "the Portland music scene. So cool you also like 90s punk rock."]

The "wrinkle" about the Portland music scene shows you took the extra ten seconds to make the email or handwritten note personal. You don't go straight for "the ask" about a job. You show interest in the other person and, in doing so, build trust.

Be on the lookout for the "wrinkle" method throughout the book and weave the strategy into your own correspondence.

Be a name dropper

Dale Carnegie, a legendary author and speaker on leadership, believed a person's name is the "sweetest and most important sound in any language."

Same goes for email. Our eyes will lock onto a message if the writer addresses us by name.

Yes, you generally open an email with a person's name:

"Hi Susan,"...

We should also include a first name in other places in the email. A "name drop" makes our message more personable and genuine.

Other opportunities to call someone out by name:

▸ When you give a compliment: "Susan, your speech today was fantastic."

▸ When you need the person to pay special attention: "Susan, please make sure you..."

▸ At the end: "Thanks again for the assistance, Susan. It means a great deal."

The "name drop." Simple, subtle and powerful all at once.

Four sneaky words that diminish our work

Pronouns are a nuisance and in particular the four in bold: **this, that, these** and **those**.

Time and again, the words create confusion and water down your message. Emails, job applications, presentations. All over the place.

Exception to every rule: Sometimes we use pronouns to tease people on purpose.

Like an email newsletter subject line that reads, "You're not gonna believe THIS one!"

Or even the title to my book: Wait, How Do I Write This Email?

Once the pronoun lures the person in, you then need to explain what "this" means. Got it?

OK, let's explore the use of pronouns in our careers. Here's an example on a cover letter.

The person starts a new paragraph with:

"One reason I did **that** is because I need the right skills to be competitive."

In the writer's mind, the sentence is fine. Of course "**that**" refers to the previous paragraph and the decision to obtain a master's of sustainable design from Big State University.

Not so fast. Readers need constant guidance and a nondescript pronoun leads them astray. The sentence should be:

"One reason I **obtained the master's degree** is because I need the right skills to be competitive."

Get my drift? Below, I have an easy way to remove the four troublesome pronouns when appropriate.

Instructions

1. Hit CTRL+F and look for the pronouns: **this, that, these** and **those**.
2. If the pronoun represents a word or phrase, consider if you should delete and replace.
   - ▸ "I wrote **that** to prove a point" becomes "I wrote **the grammar lesson** to prove a point"
   - ▸ "Sally gave me **this** to say thanks" becomes "Sally gave me **the present** to say thanks"
   - ▸ "The Millers need **these** for the vacation" becomes "The Millers need **the house keys** for the vacation"
   - ▸ "John handed me **those** to be helpful" becomes "John handed me **the hammer and nails** to be helpful"
3. Check your edits for clarity and comprehension.
4. Voila! You made your work sharper and more professional in a few quick minutes.

Chapter 2

How to Send Emails like a Pro

The Guides

AN EMAIL IS FAR MORE THAN A SIMPLE BLOCK OF TEXT FROM ONE PERSON TO ANOTHER. EVERY NEW MESSAGE IS A CHANCE TO PRESS "SEND" WITH IMPACT AND ELEVATE YOUR PROFESSIONAL REPUTATION.

In Chapter 2, we break down the typical email and rebuild it smarter and more polished. From the opening introduction to the email signature, you will view every future email in a new light.

HOW TO ADDRESS PEOPLE PROPERLY

You open a new email, click in the message area and grind to a halt.

Hmmm. How do I address this person? Do I start off with a formal title? More casual tone?

What if I use the wrong introduction? Then I could put out a weird vibe before my email is even read!

We've all been there. And it's confusing.

That's why I created a chart on how to properly address people based on your age and the nature of your relationship with the email recipient.

Use the chart when you apply for jobs, network and launch any other conversation where you need the intro to be "just right."

NOTE: If you don't know someone's age, take the safe route and use "Mr." or "Ms." Also, if a person provides a college graduation year on LinkedIn, it can sometimes help you determine his/her age.

If you're ages 18-22

Age of Email Recipient	Nature of Relationship	Title in the Email
Under 35	Never met or an acquaintance	"Hi [first name]"
Under 35	Friendly or have spoken in person	"Hi [first name]"
Over 35	Never met or an acquaintance	"Hi Mr./Ms. _____" Use "Ms." unless you know the woman wants to be addressed as "Mrs."
Over 35	Friendly or have spoken in person	"Hi [first name]"

Deeper Insight

When you're 18–22 (and likely a college student), you need to address people formally if they're over age 35. That age (35) is my benchmark for when people cross over into REAL adulthood. Translation: they have departed young adulthood and are now senior business people.

NOTE: It is generally assumed women can be addressed as "Ms." versus "Mrs."

If you're ages 23–30

Age of Email Recipient	Nature of Relationship	Title in the Email
Under 40	Never met or an acquaintance	"Hi [first name]"
Under 40	Friendly or have spoken in person	"Hi [first name]"
Over 40	Never met or an acquaintance	"Hi Mr./Ms. _____" Use "Ms." unless you know the woman wants to be addressed as "Mrs."
Over 40	Friendly or have spoken in person	"Hi [first name]"

Deeper Insight

The rules are similar to the ones for people ages 18–22, but I moved everything up by five years since you're a bit older.

If you're ages 31–40

Age of Email Recipient	Nature of Relationship	Title in the Email
Under 40	Never met or an acquaintance	"Hi [first name]"
Under 40	Friendly or have spoken in person	"Hi [first name]"
Over 40	Never met or an acquaintance	"Hi [first name]"
Over 40	Friendly or have spoken in person	"Hi [first name]"

Deeper Insight

Once you enter your 30s, most people you contact are on a first-name basis. You are now a mature working professional and don't need to add a "Mr." or "Ms." when you address people in emails.

NOTE: Exceptions to the rule: dignitaries, public officials and "important" people over age 60 (ex: you email a CEO and ask if he/she will give a commencement speech for a graduation).

If the person is a doctor, make sure to use "Dr." as a formal title.

Make your point at the beginning

With most networking emails, we need to include the "big ask."

- ▸ **Ask** for a coffee chat

- ▸ **Ask** for someone to put in a word about a job

- ▸ **Ask** a colleague to connect you to another person

The key with the "big ask": don't bury it. Otherwise, you sound like a timid rookie. ("Please, won't you help me?")

If "the ask" comes near the beginning, you seem confident and sure of yourself. ("I know what I'm doing.")

Let's say you want a meeting with a business owner to talk about freelance opportunities.

The "Bury the Lead" Version

Hi Mr. Thompson,

My name is Jane Doe, and I am a web developer who specializes in small business websites. I hope you're doing well.

For the past seven years, I have worked with various media firms in Houston to create sharp websites for a range of clients. I have completed websites for a veterinary clinic, auto body shop, 24-hour gym, family-owned grocery and a teacher's supply store.

Please see a few examples of my work down below:

- ▸ Example 1
- ▸ Example 2
- ▸ Example 3

I have reasonable rates and work quickly to finish the job. I can also provide references if you'd like.

Please let me know if we can meet and explore how I can help your team.

Thanks so much,

Jane

Explanation

Where is the "big ask" in the email? The second to last line:

Please let me know if we can meet and explore how I can help your team.

First, people are busy so Jane needs to be up front about what she wants (a meeting to explore how she can gain new business).

Second, a request at the end has a "pretty please" feel to it.

Like she's saying, "I don't know if you're busy or not but maybe you could find some time for me? K thanks bye."

Now see the email with the "big ask" higher in the message.

The "Assertive" Version

Hi Mr. Thompson,

My name is Jane Doe, and I am a web developer who specializes in small business websites. I hope you're doing well.

If possible, I'd like to explore ways I can help your team on website projects.

For the past seven years, I have worked with various media firms in Houston to create sharp websites for a range of clients. I have completed websites for a veterinary clinic, auto body shop, 24-hour gym, family-owned grocery and a teacher's supply store.

Please see a few examples of my work down below:

▸ Example 1

▸ Example 2

▸ Example 3

I have reasonable rates and work quickly to finish the job. I can also provide references if you'd like.

Please let me know if we can meet to talk further.

Thanks so much,

Jane

Explanation

Do you see the difference? Here, the "big ask" comes in line two:

If possible, I'd like to explore ways I can help your team on website projects.

Right away, the reader knows Jane wants a meeting to discuss freelance opportunities. Then, the rest of the email underscores why she deserves one.

The "big ask" at the beginning is direct and *feels* more confident. Also, it shows Jane values someone's time. As in, "I know you're busy. Let me get right to the point."

Remember, don't bury the lead. Put it right where people can see it.

Careful with acronyms

Since *Wait, How Do I Write This Email?* is all about brevity, acronyms might seem like a smart idea. What an easy way to trim the word count, right?

Sorry, that's not the case.

Let's say you're a researcher for a pharmaceutical company and work in a division called RDT. You use the expression "RDT" 25 times a day, and to you the acronym obviously means "Research and Development Team."

To anyone outside of your team — possibly at the same company — RDT means... well, nothing.

Every time you include an acronym in an email — or resume, cover letter and presentation — you must follow one basic rule:

32

Provide the full name of the acronym on first reference.

For instance:

This week I can report on a major success from the RDT (Research and Development Team). After many months of testing, we have now determined...

Then, the reader understands what RDT means, and all future references can be "RDT" on its own.

One more example, this time from a cover letter:

In 2012, I worked as a FA (field associate) for Big Nonprofit and studied the impact of a power plant on the James River in Virginia. As an FA, I found the job challenging because...

> NOTE: Of course, there are exceptions to every rule:
>
> Some acronyms are commonly known and don't need an explanation. For example: ABC, NBC, CBS, NFL, USPS, UPS and AT&T. When you write an acronym, ask yourself if the average person would know what it means. If the answer is "no" or "I'm not sure," provide the full title.
>
> An informed reader = a happy reader.

Let the words breathe

Here's what happens when you write a long email. At first, the reader is with you and can follow each word without much strain. A few sentences, no big deal. Then, as you continue, the tune changes. The paragraph grows longer, and the reader begins to think, "OK, this is getting to be a bit much." Still, the paragraph keeps going and becomes not only cumbersome but also problematic. Nowadays, we communicate in tweets and texts, and the mere sight of a big chunk of words makes us groan and wonder, "Do I REALLY need to read the entire thing? Ugh." We feel transported back to sophomore year of college and 19th Century British Literature, the class with such dense reading you wanted to pull the eyes from your head. We almost never make it to the last line, which means we don't follow the writer from start to finish. That's a shame because the last line contains the most important advice: people will read every sentence if the words have room to breathe.

Let's try the paragraph again, and you will see what I mean:

Here's what happens when you write a big email.

At first, the reader is with you and can follow each word without much strain. A few sentences, no big deal.

Then, as you continue, the tune changes. The paragraph grows longer, and the reader begins to think, "OK, this is getting to be a bit much."

Still, the paragraph keeps going and becomes not only cumbersome but also problematic. Nowadays, we communicate in tweets and texts, and the mere sight of a big chunk of words makes us groan and wonder, "Do I REALLY need to read the entire thing? Ugh."

We feel transported back to sophomore year of college and 19th Century British Literature, the class with such dense reading you wanted to pull the eyes from your head.

We almost never make it to the last line, which means we don't follow the writer from start to finish.

That's a shame because the last line contains the most important advice: people will read every sentence if the words have room to breathe.

––––––

Am I right? Did you read from start to finish? Thought so.

Turn bulky paragraphs into breezy sentences.

Readers everywhere will thank you.

Seven words you should not capitalize

Capitalization matters. When you understand how to use upper and lowercase words, it shows poise, smarts and maturity.

NOTE: I know a lot of words like "Political Science Major" feel important, but editing has strict rules; there's no room for feelings.

Here are seven types of words we need to stop capitalizing.

1. Job titles

Incorrect: I am a Marketing Coordinator at Acme Corporation.

Correct: I am a marketing coordinator at Acme Corporation.

Explanation: Job titles are lowercase unless they come before your name (ex: Marketing Coordinator Jane Doe is...).

2. College majors

Incorrect: In college, I Majored in Political Science and Minored in Religious Studies.

Correct: In college, I majored in political science and minored in religious studies.

Explanation: College majors and minors are lowercase — even the words "major" and "minor." Uppercase comes into play if you describe the actual program/school (ex: I studied political science at the John Doe School of Public Affairs at Big State University).

3. Special occasions

Incorrect: *Classic Facebook post* — Thanks to everyone for the Birthday wishes!

Correct: Thanks to everyone for the birthday wishes!

Explanation: Words like birthday, anniversary, reunion and gala are lowercase. If you describe an event with a proper name (Lizzy's Surprise 30th Birthday Bash), then it's uppercase.

4. Important-sounding career words

Incorrect: *Common phrase in a resume objective statement* — Experienced Team Leader with strong Organizational Skills and a Successful career in Management.

Correct: Experienced team leader with strong organizational skills and a successful career in management.

Explanation: We don't capitalize non-specific career words no matter how important they seem ("Successful"). If you attend the Acme Team Leader Training Seminar, then the words are uppercase because they're a proper name.

5. Seasons

Incorrect: I began at Acme Corporation in the Fall of 2012.

Correct: I began at Acme Corporation in the fall of 2012.

Explanation: Seasons are lowercase unless part of a proper title (ex: Fall Fling Art Show).

6. Directions

Incorrect: After college, I headed West to Los Angeles to pursue acting.

Correct: After college, I headed west to Los Angeles to pursue acting.

Explanation: Directions are lowercase. If you write about a specific part of the country, then it's uppercase ("live on the East Coast").

7. Any other word that feels special but isn't a proper noun

Your time at the political internship made a big impact on your career. Great. That doesn't mean you had an Internship. Nope, it's still an *internship*. It's not a proper noun.

However, if you write about your experience in the Acme Collegiate Internship Program, then "Internship" is capitalized because it's part of a proper title.

Capitalization is a small detail, I know. But then again, the little stuff often makes the biggest difference.

How to craft an effective email signature

As your career evolves, so does your email signature. You might go from college student to unemployed to employed to graduate student and then to employed again.

At each stop, how should you display contact info at the bottom of an email?

On the following pages, you will find templates for the different phases of our young professional lives. Before you begin, heed these four rules:

▸ Remember: less is more. You don't need to give people nine ways to contact you. Focus on the best ones (ex: phone, email, Twitter and LinkedIn) and make it easy on you and them.

▸ Stay away from a signature that's one big image. Keep it as text so email services won't block people from seeing it.

▸ Make links long enough so they're easy to click on a smartphone.

▸ Include your #personalhashtag when appropriate, as we discuss on page 50. The hashtag lets you give people a quick look at your background and interests. Better yet: link people to your blog or portfolio. A website is more impressive so if you have one, include it.

> NOTE: If you're not on Twitter, you need to be. It's a terrific place to network, make connections and showcase who you are. All of my templates in this chapter involve Twitter. It's time you join the party.

Let's follow the life of a fictional person named Amanda Garcia, a college student who hopes to work in graphic design.

Email signature for a full-time college student

Your Name
TITLE, STUDENT ORGANIZATION

COLLEGE OR UNIVERSITY, CLASS OF _____

EMAIL | CELL: XXX-XXX-XXXX

TWITTER | #YOURNAMEPORTFOLIO

EXAMPLE:

Amanda Garcia
VICE PRESIDENT, STUDENT GOVERNMENT ASSOCIATION

BIG STATE UNIVERSITY, CLASS OF 2019

XXXX@_____.EDU | CELL: 555-555-5555

TWITTER | #AMANDAGARCIAPORTFOLIO

Explanation:

The college student signature lets Amanda cover a lot of territory in five lines. She provides her role in a student organization, school, the year she will graduate and contact information. She also includes a personal hashtag so people can learn more about her recent projects, interests and articles she enjoyed (#amandagarciaportfolio).

If Amanda has a blog or portfolio, she can replace the personal hashtag:

TWITTER | MY PORTFOLIO: AMANDA GARCIA DESIGNS

OK, Amanda graduated and finds herself in the harsh real world with no job. Womp.

What now? How does her email signature adjust?

Email signature for a working professional (need a job)

Your Name

EMAIL | CELL: XXX-XXX-XXXX

TWITTER | LINKEDIN | #YOURNAMEPORTFOLIO

EXAMPLE:

Amanda Garcia

XXXX@GMAIL.COM I CELL: 555-555-5555

TWITTER | LINKEDIN | #AMANDAGARCIAPORTFOLIO

Explanation:

Need a job? OK, let's tighten everything up. Amanda gives people her basic contact info (email, cell, Twitter and LinkedIn). She also includes the personal hashtag, in which she shares her artwork and creative projects as she wants a job in graphic design. Amanda makes it easy for employers to view her skills and expertise.

If Amanda has a blog or portfolio, she can replace the personal hashtag:

TWITTER | LINKEDIN | MY PORTFOLIO: AMANDA GARCIA DESIGNS

Hooray! Amanda's hard work, persistence and clever personal marketing (#amandagarciaportfolio) paid off. She now has a job and is ready to tell…well, everyone who reads the bottom of her emails. Proudly, Amanda updates her email signature with the fresh new job title.

Email signature for a working professional (with a job)

Your Name

TITLE, COMPANY

EMAIL I CELL: XXX-XXX-XXXX (INCLUDE OFFICE LINE, IF NECESSARY)

TWITTER I LINKEDIN I #YOURNAMEPORTFOLIO

COMPANY URL

EXAMPLE:

Amanda Garcia

ASSISTANT CREATIVE DIRECTOR, ACME CORPORATION

XXXX@_____.COM I CELL: 555-555-5555

TWITTER I LINKEDIN I #AMANDAGARCIAPORTFOLIO

ACME CORPORATION

Explanation:

The above is a universal template for a professional email signature. Your company could require all kinds of specifics in the signature including a slogan, link to a landing page and additional phone numbers. The template here is a starting point.

Note Amanda still includes her personal hashtag. Now, she produces work for Acme and can use the hashtag to promote recent company projects and successes. The hashtag #amandagarciaportfolio is an ever-evolving place to highlight her latest and greatest achievements — personal or professional.

Email signature if you work and go to graduate school

Your Name

TITLE, COMPANY

EMAIL I CELL: XXX-XXX-XXXX (INCLUDE OFFICE LINE, IF NECESSARY)

TWITTER | LINKEDIN | #YOURNAMEPORTFOLIO

COMPANY URL

[DEGREE] CANDIDATE, [DEGREE PROGRAM][SEASON, YEAR] — COLLEGE OR UNIVERSITY

EXAMPLE:

Amanda Garcia

ASSISTANT CREATIVE DIRECTOR, ACME CORPORATION

XXXX@_____.COM I CELL: 555-555-5555

TWITTER I LINKEDIN I #AMANDAGARCIAPORTFOLIO

ACME CORPORATION

MASTER'S CANDIDATE, PROJECT MANAGEMENT (SPRING 2021) — TECH UNIVERSITY

Explanation:

Amanda decides to head back to school for a master's while she works and needs a signature to reflect both responsibilities. The easiest and cleanest way is to focus on her job first and add graduate information at the end.

Email signature for a full-time graduate student

Your Name

TITLE, DEGREE PROGRAM

COLLEGE OR UNIVERSITY, CLASS OF _____

EMAIL I CELL: XXX-XXX-XXXX

TWITTER I LINKEDIN I #YOURNAMEPORTFOLIO

EXAMPLE:

Amanda Garcia

MASTER'S STUDENT, PROJECT MANAGEMENT

TECH UNIVERSITY, CLASS OF 2021

XXXX@_____.EDU I CELL: 555-555-5555

TWITTER I LINKEDIN I #AMANDAGARCIAPORTFOLIO

Explanation:

Let's say Amanda decides to go back to graduate school full time. Now her signature is 100 percent focused on college life. Amanda also continues to update her personal hashtag, but if she maintains a portfolio, then it can replace the hashtag.

TWITTER I LINKEDIN I MY PORTFOLIO: AMANDA GARCIA DESIGNS

Assume the person might forward your email

Email has a mind all its own.

A single message can travel from one inbox to another with lightning speed, and before you know it, a note to a friend lands on someone's screen across town or around the globe.

Once you press "Send" you lose all control. That's why you should write every career-related email with the expectation the reader will forward it along.

Say you want a job at a company where your friend works. You send an email to poke around and see if the opportunity is worth it. You draft an email like this:

Hi _____,

I see Acme Corporation is a hiring a new project manager. Do you have any information on the position? Think it's something I should consider?

Let me know. Thanks!

– Your first name

What if your friend is best buds with the hiring manager? The friend might LOVE for you to work at Acme and could forward along your info. Problem is, your email is weak, weak, weak. It has no substance, no details.

Even though your friend might know all about your career, remember the "forward" concept in case the email grows legs and travels.

Hi _____,

I see Acme Corporation is a hiring a new project manager. I'm interested in the job and think I would be a great fit. As you know, I have solid experience that aligns with the job.

– I worked for the past three years at Big Corporation as a project manager and also conducted marketing for new mobile phone plans.

– I received a master's in information systems from Big State University while at Big Corporation.

– I began a "startup" lab inside Big Corporation and developed new video chat tools for internal communications, which boosted employee engagement.

Let me know if you have any insight into the project manager position. I would be happy to send my resume to the right person.

Thanks a lot,

– Your first name

Sure, your friend knows about your master's degree, but the employer who might also see your email has no idea — and will be impressed by it.

The "forward" rule is the reason you must provide concrete information about your career and include an example of how you solved a problem (ex: created video chat tools to improve employee engagement). The email then does the selling before you ever send a resume or utter a word.

Finish out every conversation

You know what's annoying? When you send someone a message with important information, and the person never responds.

Then, you sit around and wonder, "Did she see my email? Did it go to spam? Do I need to send it again?"

A quick "Thanks. I got it." and all those questions disappear. Message received. Case closed.

The best communicators fire off notes every day like "Thanks," "OK sure," and "Same to you." When it feels like an email deserves a response — even a small

43

one — they take three seconds and knock it out. The strategy of finishing every email conversation makes you look poised, responsible and on your game.

Three email examples

YOU: I'll plan to meet you tomorrow at 3:30 p.m. near the sound stage, and we'll make sure everything is set for the speech at 5 p.m. Cool?

OTHER PERSON: Sounds good. I'll be there at 3:30 p.m.

YOU: Great, thanks.

If you didn't finish out the conversation with "Great, thanks." the person might wonder, "Did she see my last email? Does she know I'll be at the sound stage at 3:30 p.m.?"

Again, your quick reply makes all the difference.

YOU: Nice work this past week on the Sinclair account. That was a big job, but we got it done in time. Thanks again.

OTHER PERSON: You're welcome. Thanks for your help pushing the project along. Enjoy the holidays and all the best to your family.

YOU: Same to you. Happy Holidays.

The person gave you a little "best wishes" for your family. If you let the email chain die right there, the person might think, "Hmm, did he see my last email? Why didn't he say 'Same to you'? Maybe he's a little annoyed with me?"

Don't make people play the guessing game. Finish every email conversation. Stay in the moment.

YOU: My plane arrives in Dallas at 4 p.m. so I should make it to the conference by 5 p.m. or so, depending on traffic. I'll let you know when I land.

YOUR BOSS: OK sounds good. The conference doesn't get going until dinner at 6 so you should be fine.

YOU: Great. Glad I won't miss anything.

The strategy of finishing every email chain is essential with management. Make sure the boss knows you read each message.

You're not too busy. You're not too important.

Take a few seconds and conclude every email conversation. You give the other person peace of mind, demonstrate maturity and earn respect. All from a simple thank you.

What could be easier?

Next-Level Techniques

READY TO STEP UP YOUR EMAIL GAME?

In "Next-Level Techniques," we explore advanced topics to give our messages another layer of impact.

Keep your thinking cap on. We're almost done with the email lessons and ready to move into the templates.

WHEN TO USE EXCLAMATION POINTS IN WORK EMAILS

Back in the day, the rules were simple.

In the office? Suit and tie. Write a memo? Keep it formal.

Today, social mores have changed and the default setting is often business casual. That applies to everything from the clothes we wear to how we communicate. Does that mean it's OK to fill our emails with exclamation points? I say no.

Yes, we glide from Gmail to Twitter to Gchat and the messages muddle together, but work email should still be seen as "professional." Too many exclamation marks imply you're young and inexperienced. Right or wrong, they make people question your seriousness. After you've been in a position for a few months and see your colleagues, including your manager, sprinkle exclamation marks into every message, then you can relax a bit.

I'm not so rigid to suggest we never use an exclamation mark! As in all things, moderation is key.

I. Hello and Goodbye

Let's start where all emails begin: the introduction. Plenty of people open a work email with:

Hi_____,

Good morning!

They also end with:

Have a great day!

Exclamation marks at the beginning and end. No big deal.
The other half of the population goes with:

Hi_____,

Good morning.

And for the finish…

Have a great day.

Which one is right? They both are. Intros and outros are the entrance and exit of the conversation. They are only pleasantries so, yes, you can come and go with an energetic tone (!) or something more subdued. Either way, it's not a distraction to the reader.

II. Let the Other Person Make the First Move

Now we depart the safe harbor of the email introduction (where the exclamation mark is up to you) and enter the body of our message. Here's where exclamations are a far riskier game.

If you already led with:

Hi_____,

Good morning!

Then you might think you can continue to roll with the excited streak:

I want to send an email to catch everyone up on the project since we have a lot going on! Please respond that you saw this email so I know you're in the loop!

And the reader thinks:

"Yikes, calm down over there. It's Monday morning, and I haven't even finished my coffee."

So let's make a new plan. Rather than start off strong with exclamations, let other people make the first move and match *their* emotion. That way, you're always in line with how they want to exchange messages.

If the person writes back:

Thanks so much for the note!

Then you reply:

> You're welcome!

If the person goes with:

> Thanks so much for the note.

Then you reply:

> You're welcome.

When you defer to other people, you're always right. If they want to drop exclamations here and there, so do you. If they prefer to keep it plain, you feel the same way.

III. Double Exclamations

In parts I and II, I make the case you can go either way with exclamation marks. In part III, the tune changes.

> *NOTE: Double exclamations have no place in a work email. I make no apologies for that rule.*

There's a difference between energetic and overkill, and it happens somewhere between ! and !!

If you're on Gchat or talking to a friend through Gmail, go nuts!!!

But when it comes to work, the double exclamation is double trouble. Remember you're a working professional. Business is business. Money is money.

You need people to feel comfortable using you or you firm. If you drop !! into every sentence, it could be seen as a red flag.

IV. When an Exclamation is Necessary

Part IV is where you "learn the rules and break them." That's because there are situations where an exclamation mark matters even if you don't like to use one.

Hey there,

I want to tell you I landed the promotion so now I'm VP of development for the entire East Coast. Thought you'd like to know the good news!

That's a pretty big deal, right? You can't come back with:

That's great news. Congrats.

Your answer does not match the person's emotion. The moment deserves:

That's great news! Congrats!

If you want the person to know how excited you are, then you need an exclamation mark. If the person wrote the big email to a group, everyone may respond with:

Amazing!

Congrats! Woohoo!

Incredible!

There's no way you could drop in with:

Congrats.

Now you appear unenthusiastic and as though you sent good wishes through gritted teeth.

Some moments require you to fall in line.

V. Trust Your Instincts

When you finish composing an email, look over your work. How many exclamation points have you used?

If it "feels" like you overdid it, then you overdid it. That applies even if you try to keep pace with the other person's use of exclamations.

No matter what, you never want to appear *less* professional than the person on the other end.

You want to be...what's the word?

Ah, yes.

Appropriate.

Why you don't add the email address until you're ready to send

Here's a common situation. You click "Send" on accident while you're in the middle of a sentence. Then you need to write back awkwardly and say, "Sorry, didn't mean to hit send yet!"

Even worse, you could write an angry email to let off steam but never intend to go through with it. But if the email address is already in there and you mistakenly press "Send"...oops.

I know with my Gmail account I have a few seconds to "Undo" a message and bring it back to "Draft" status, but that's a dangerous game when the clock is ticking.

Here's the order to follow:

1. Subject line
2 Email body
3. Attachments
4. Recipient's email address

Once you add the email address, it's the signal to your brain that says, "This message is ready to go." You are comfortable with the content and how the other person will perceive it. It's like the final walk-through before a NASA launch.

Otherwise, an email riddled with errors or one that's inappropriate could land in someone's inbox and make your life miserable.

> NOTE: To be certain an email is "ready," review the message for grammar and clarity. Should someone else look over the email too? If it's an extra important email, leave it in "Draft" overnight and make final tweaks the next day.

Why you need a #personalhashtag

Remember when the "pound" sign was exclusively a tease for more information on social media? If we searched the particular hashtag, we would find more content related to the word or phrase.

Now, we post a Facebook photo of a shiny diamond ring and tag it with:

#OMGcantbelieveimengaged #loveatfirstsight #isaidYES

Without warning, the hashtag has morphed into an amusing way to describe our mood or the moment. We need to tell the world how we feel, and a hashtag seems the snappiest way to do it.

#notimeforacompletesentence

Hang on a second. What if our unique hashtags could revolutionize the idea of a resume and professional portfolio?

#whoa

Introducing the #PersonalHashtag campaign

Let's say you send out dozens of resumes as you look in every direction for a job. Right below your name, you add a personal hashtag so the resume stands out (for an example, check out #dannyrubinportfolio). You also include the hashtag at the top of cover letters and in your email signature.

Employers are likely to stop cold and check out your hashtag.

Why? Because they've never seen anything like it.

With a personal hashtag campaign, you share what an employer needs to see.

#whatasimpleidea

Think about it. An employer reads so many nearly identical resumes that his eyes start to roll into the back of his head. All of a sudden, he notices a personal hashtag in the corner of yours. He's intrigued. He jumps on Twitter, types in your hashtag and finds a neat little list of your work accomplishments or other notable achievements.

> NOTE: You should not include inappropriate content, photos and conversations that are purely social, celebrity gossip or contain foul language. Keep the hashtag professional.

Before long, the employer clicks around and learns about you while everyone else is lost in the mountain of resumes on his desk.

#victoryisyours

Even if you have a secure position and no plans to quit, a hashtag like #yournameportfolio is an ongoing glimpse into your world. You can link people to:

- a big project you finished
- a website you maintain or a personal one that serves as a portfolio
- an article that mentions you or one you find interesting
- community or volunteer organizations you're involved with
- your company's services or roster of clients

You then have a live portfolio accessible to anyone on the planet. Plus, you can switch out the info whenever you want. A person only needs to stumble upon **#yournameportfolio** (or whatever you choose to call it), and — bam — you are on full display.

#onelessreasonforpaper #savintrees

What will you call your #personalhashtagcampaign? And what will you share?

In business today, you need to tell your story faster and smarter than the next person.

#getwhatsyours

Chart: How long to wait before a follow-up email

How many times have you sent an email and waited…and waited…and waited for a response?

All the time, right? Like every single day. You're anxious, want an answer and are tempted to send the "Did you see my email?" message right away.

Not so fast. I created a chart to show the appropriate waiting periods for the follow-up email in various career situations.

Visit page 93 for the template on how to check in when the person doesn't respond in a timely manner.

Career Challenge	Amount of Time	Additional Notes
Need an urgent response	Give person 1–2 hours to respond. If no answer, it's time to check in.	We all have smartphones today and see email immediately. If a person knows you need a response ASAP, then you have every right to follow up within 1–2 hours.
Wait on an update	Wait 24 hours for the update. If it never comes, send another email.	Don't jump down the person's throat looking for the info. Let your request simmer, and after a day has passed check back in.
Wait on someone to network for you	Let 2–3 days go by.	Someone has offered to do you a favor. Great. So give it time, and let the person fit the "free" help into his/her own schedule.
Send an email about doing business with someone new	Let 2–3 days go by.	If no answer after the follow-up email, then the person might not be interested. You can either wait a week and email again or if you feel it's appropriate, pick up the phone and reach the person that way.
Wait for confirmation after you send a job application	Let 2–3 days go by.	2–3 days is enough time to receive a "Thanks, we have your application." For the follow-up email template, turn to page 128.

OK, great work. You've reached the end of the writing and email lessons. I'm sure your brain is full, but stay with me. Now it's time to push into the world of email templates. First up is networking situations.

Onward!

Chapter 3

Networking Templates

General Networking

In the following chapters, I strip effective networking down to its core: a natural curiosity in someone else.

We often think the best networkers are people who talk about themselves with ease and deal out business cards as if they work in a Vegas casino.

Yes, it's important to tell our story and promote ourselves — and we cover that topic too. Still, the smartest networkers understand they must first take an interest in other people's lives and careers. They inquire, probe, explore and give more than they get.

Selflessness is the secret sauce to an enduring business relationship.

HOW TO SET UP A NETWORKING MEETING

We begin our templates with an old standard: the traditional networking meeting.

If you want to make introductions, discuss a project, explore job opportunities or meet for another reason altogether, the template below will allow you to start the conversation.

Subject line: Interested in connecting

Hi _____,

My name is [first and last name], and I am [reason you know the person/ reason you want to meet; for instance, "the son of Jim Reeves, your former co-worker" or "a recent grad from Big State University with a degree in computer science"]. I hope you're doing well.

[Then, the reason you want to meet; for instance, "As I'm new to the job market, I hope we can meet for coffee so I can learn more about your career and job prospects in the field of animation."]

> NOTE: Ask to meet early in the email so the person knows what you
> want right away.

[Then, prove you did your research on the person through a company website bio or LinkedIn profile; for instance, "I checked out your bio and see you have a lot of design experience, particularly from your time in Hollywood on big budget animated films. That must have been a fantastic opportunity."]

> NOTE: Take the time to understand the other person's career.
> He/she will appreciate your interest and often be more willing
> to respond.

To give you my quick background, I [one to two highlights from your resume that would matter to this person; for instance, "recently completed an internship at Acme Corporation, in which I was able to use the software programs XXXX and XXXX. Here's a link to my latest animated work"].

Again, it would be great to meet with you in person. Please let me know your availability over the next couple of weeks.

Thanks, [person's first name]. I look forward to talking with you.

– Your first name

Email signature

Deeper Insight

Notice how the template includes details in two key places.

1. Interest in the other person's career ("big budget animated films")
2. Explanation of your own career ("was able to use the software programs…")

The information makes you interesting and goes a long way when you write to someone for the first time.

Also, note how you ask for an in-person meeting rather than a phone call. Why? You will develop a stronger relationship if you physically make introductions.

How to send a thank-you note after a networking meeting

Within 24 hours of your networking meeting, you need to send a thank-you email. It's not enough to say "Thanks so much" when you're in the room with the person. The email cements how much you appreciate the person's time and also gives you the opportunity to continue the conversation.

Subject line: Thanks again for the meeting

Hi _____,

Thank you again for meeting with me [earlier today/yesterday] at [place where you met]. I appreciate your time and the advice you passed along. [Then a quick piece of advice that stuck with you; for instance, "You're 100 percent correct about how I should explore business opportunities in the city's tech sector. I had not considered that route but I will now."]

[Then include a detail about the other person's world to prove you listened; for instance, "And I can tell from our conversation you're excited about Acme Corporation and what's on tap for the company next year. Good luck with everything."]

[If the person has offered to pass along your resume, include, "I have attached my resume here. Please feel free to cc me on any emails, and I am happy to follow up myself."]

> NOTE: Always offer to be copied on networking emails so you can jump in, take over and politely remove your networker from the conversation if/when appropriate.

[If you don't need a job, you might want to end the email with an idea to push the relationship further; for instance, "Yes, I'd be happy to drop by your office and meet the team. I think there may be some ways we can all work together on the upcoming campaign. Let me know a good day/time."]

Thanks again, [person's first name]. Have a great day.

– Your first name

Email signature

Deeper Insight

Show the person you value his/her advice. In fact, you find the person's wisdom SO notable you repeated it back in your thank-you email. That's a major ego boost and added incentive for the person to pass along your resume, meet up again or send networking emails on your behalf.

How to inquire about freelance opportunities

You have skills that companies need. Now's the time to send a polished email to make introductions and spark a new relationship.

Subject line: [Your job title; for instance, "Website developer,"] interested in freelance opportunities

Hi _____,

My name is [first and last name], and I am a [job title and your expertise; for instance, a "web developer who specializes in small business websites"]. I hope you're doing well.

I'd like to explore ways I can help your team on [however you can add value; for instance, "website projects"]. I checked out [name of company's] website and like the work you do, in particular [name two projects and provide links; for instance, "the landing page for the Acme Hospital System and the ecommerce site for the rental car startup. You produce high quality work, and I respect your attention to detail"].

> NOTE: Provide examples of the company's work and explain WHY you appreciate it. The details show you care what the team is all about.

For the past _____ years, I have worked with [talk about your experience so far and list examples of past clients; for instance, "various media firms in Santa Monica to create sharp websites for a range of clients. I have completed websites for a gymnastics training center, CPA firm, environmental nonprofit and a senior living community"].

Please see a few examples of my work down below:

– [link to examples of your work, if available]

– Example #2

– Example #3

> NOTE: You can also attach files if it makes more sense.

I have reasonable rates and always meet my deadlines. I can also provide references if you'd like.

Please let me know if we can talk further.

Thanks so much,

– Your first name

Email signature

Deeper insight

Too many freelancers forget the email template isn't about them. In fact, the freelancer needs to prove how much he/she values the company and the work it does.

In other words, demonstrate you didn't send the exact same email to 20 companies. Do your homework, offer compliments and take an interest in others so they will want to take an interest in you.

How to congratulate someone on a job well done

Want a quick, easy way to build a relationship? Send people short notes because they did something great. No strings attached. No fine print.

'Tis better to give than receive, right?

Subject line: Great job with [particular project; for instance, "the LinkedIn workshop"]

Hi _____,

You did an excellent job when you [specific project; for instance, "led the team in the day-long workshop on LinkedIn strategies"].

> NOTE: Don't write "Nice work!" No, tell the person exactly why you think he/she did so well.

In particular, I like how you [again, be specific; for instance, "took the extra time to help Jim figure out how to fix his profile photo. One day he'll understand all these social media tools"].

Thanks for all of your efforts. I'm sure it took a lot of preparation, but you made it look easy.

Have a great day!

– Your first name

Deeper Insight

A thank-you note is nice. A thank-you note with specific references is even better.

In my example, the line about Jim's profile photo proves you watched your co-worker and made particular note of why he/she did so well. The attention to detail will go a long, long way.

How to tell your network you're looking for new opportunities

You're a free agent in the job market. Now it's time to tap your network and see who knows who. The best way? An email (or Facebook/LinkedIn post) to spread the word — professionally.

Subject line: Making moves in my career

Hi everyone,

As some of you know, I have [recently graduated from _____/left my job at _____ and am looking for career opportunities].

[If you feel it's necessary to explain why you left your job, do so here; for instance, "Acme Corporation had a recent round of layoffs and unfortunately I was part of the downsizing."]

> NOTE: It's often a smart idea to explain why you're out in the job market. Otherwise, people will respond to your email and want to know if everything is OK. You should avoid those awkward questions as much as possible.

[Then, give people an idea of the job you hope to find; for instance, "I will keep my search broad and am interested in jobs in marketing or sales. I have experience in both fields and want to have as many options as possible."]

[Then, two quick bullets on your experience; for instance:

– At Acme, I handled marketing for the company, which included three different email newsletter campaigns to an audience of 47,000 people.

– At the job, I also worked with the sales team to pitch new products like cordless hand tools and rechargeable batteries.]

> NOTE: Don't go too deeply into your experience here and give out numbers or data your past employers might not want to make public. Offer your network a quick idea of what you did so others can think about you for similar work. In a one-on-one conversation, you can then discuss your accomplishments in depth.

[Then, explain your geographical parameters; for instance, "I hope to find a job here in the Birmingham area but would consider a move if the opportunity is right."]

I have attached my resume to the email. Please let me know if you can connect me with any job opportunities.

Thanks so much,

– Your first name

Email signature

Deeper Insight

If you're a recent grad, include examples of your experience at internships or at college. Don't tell people you "interned at _____." That's not good enough. Write about an actual project you worked on like, "As an intern at _____, I attended client events like _____ and wrote social media posts about _____."

You might want to include other details in the email — you know your network better than anyone else — but the parts I suggest are the essentials.

How to reconnect with a friend or colleague

It's tough to check in with someone from "way back when." I hope the email below helps you through the awkwardness and rekindles the conversation.

Subject line: Hoping to reconnect

Hi _____,

Long time no talk! I hope you're doing well.

[Ask a couple of questions about the person's life and be specific; for instance, "How's your job going? Still branch manager in Tulsa? I see photos of your kids on Facebook. Is Devin doing well in school?"]

[Then, a quick update on your own life; for instance, "I'm doing great over here in Bridgeport. Work is busy as ever, and now I'm thinking about night school for my MBA."]

If you have time, it would be great for us to catch up properly over the phone. Are you free this week or next?

> NOTE: If you want to talk about something specific, drop the line here; for instance, "I have a project on the horizon where I might need your help. I can explain further over the phone."

Please let me know and talk to you soon,

– Your first name

Email signature

Deeper Insight

Start with a little small talk (What's up with you? I'm doing great) and then ask for a phone call.

It's a short and sweet re-introduction to kickstart the conversation.

QUICK TIP — "Ten Commandments" of networking emails

I, Danny Rubin, hereby set forth ten commandments for emails of the networking variety.

I. Be courteous — "I hope you're doing well."

II. Be grateful — "Thanks for any help you can offer."

III. Be curious — "I checked out your website and read about your recent project on employee behavior. Was it a challenge to complete the survey?"

IV. Be clear — "I'm a friend of Robert Holland, your former co-worker at Acme Corporation."

V. Be considerate — "I know you're busy, and I appreciate your time."

VI.   Be direct — "I'm writing to see if you're free for coffee."

VII.   Be honest — "I'm a recent grad and would appreciate learning from you."

VIII.   Be patient — "Please let me know when you have a chance."

IX.   Be careful — No spelling or grammar mistakes; first impressions are huge.

X.   Be bold — Send an email and start the conversation. Nothing ventured, nothing gained.

Networking Events/Groups

HOW TO WRITE SOMEONE FROM A NETWORKING EVENT ABOUT A JOB

You met someone at a networking event or happy hour who may be able to connect you with a job opportunity. Terrific. Now what should you do? Send an email within 24 hours to keep the momentum going.

Subject line: Follow up from [name of networking event; for instance, "Rising Leaders Happy Hour"]

Hi _____,

It was great to meet you [earlier today/yesterday] at the [name of networking event]. I enjoyed our conversation about [reference a part of your discussion; for instance, "the Portland music scene. So cool you also like 90s punk rock"].

NOTE: Be personable and prove you're a good listener.

After I left, I did more research on [either the person's company or a company the person can connect you to]. I am interested in [name of company] and especially a project like [reference a recent project from the company website and why you find it notable; for instance, "the fun recycling program with the hashtag #gogreenportland. That's the kind of creative, digital campaign I want to work on"].

65

NOTE: Always assume the person could forward the email to someone else. That's why it's important to use an example from the company's website. What if the person behind the #gogreenportland campaign sees your email? That could happen.

As I mentioned at the [name of networking event], I am a [who you are in context; for instance, "recent graduate from Big State University with a degree in marketing. I also completed an internship with Acme Corporation, in which I worked on a social media campaign for Acme in Central America"].

NOTE: Again, include a concrete example in case the person forwards the email and provide a link to the example, if available.

Please let me know if you're able to pass my resume to the right person. I have attached it to this email.

Or if you want to give me an email address of a contact, I can handle the introduction myself.

Thanks again,

– Your first name

Email signature

___

Deeper Insight

Offer to write the networking introduction yourself. The person might be happy to make an introduction but at least you took away the burden in case he/she is swamped with work.

How to write someone from a networking event about new business

If you think there's a way to work together, send an email within 24 hours to explain more about your business or project — and provide links when possible.

Subject line: Follow up from [name of networking event; for instance, "Young Pros Happy Hour"]

Hi _____,

It was great to meet you [earlier today/yesterday] at the [name of networking event]. I enjoyed our conversation about [reference a part of your discussion; for instance, "the ups and downs of the real estate industry here in Dayton. You certainly have a strong handle on the market"].

NOTE: Drop in a little small talk. Don't go right into business.

I'd like to continue the conversation and explore ways our companies can work together.

Here are a few examples of recent projects we completed at [name of your company].

– [link to your projects or work experience, if available; for instance, "Acme Shopping Center renovation"]

– Project #2

– Project #3

NOTE: If you have links available, take the extra two minutes to provide them so the person can fully understand your skills.

As you can see, we have completed a good amount of work with [the niche or field the other person would find relevant; for instance, "the redesign of existing shopping centers in western Ohio"].

Are you available to meet over the next week? If so, please let me know a time that works.

> NOTE: Give the person plenty of options to find a convenient day and time. A week is generally enough for planning purposes.

Thanks, and I hope to hear from you.

– Your first name

Email signature

Deeper Insight

There are many reasons to email someone after a networking event in the pursuit of new business or opportunities. Whatever the case, it's essential you include links to your work. That's why I preach the value of a blog or online portfolio. It's a huge advantage to have work samples whenever you need them.

How to follow up if a person handed you a business card

If someone interesting gave you a business card and you'd like to stay in touch, send an email the same week. It's a smart way to share contact info and further the conversation.

We pass out business cards all the time but rarely expect people to do anything with them — except probably throw them out. Follow up with a polished email, make a friend and expand your network.

Subject line: Nice to meet you at [name of networking event; for instance, "the chamber of commerce dinner series"]

Hi _____,

It was great to meet you [earlier today/yesterday] at the [name of networking event]. I enjoyed our conversation about [reference a part of your discussion; for instance, "your plans to expand your pet store business. It's exciting when you can feel momentum and know it's the right time to grow"].

I passed along my contact information (see my email signature) so you'll have it.

NOTE: The next section of the email depends on the nature of the conversation.

[If you want to do business with the person, reference the services you offer like, "As I said last night, we specialize in signage and banners and would be happy to help as you open a second pet store location."]

[Or maybe the person can connect you to a job. Then you could write something like, "You mentioned you have a friend at Acme Corporation. I plan to apply for a job there and would appreciate an introduction. Are you able to connect me with your friend at Acme over email?"]

[Or let's say you think the person might have a freelance opportunity for you. Then, send over links to your recent work. See the template on page 59 for details.]

Thanks so much and have a great day,

– Your first name

Email signature

Deeper Insight

In your email, be sure to reference a moment from your conversation (looks impressive), provide contact info (necessary) and give a quick pitch whether you offer business services or need a job (the person's call to action).

Don't forget you can also send the email to help the other person make new connections or grow a business. Doesn't always have to be about you. Give more than you get.

How to join networking groups in your community

Wherever we land, we need a job and perhaps a community of like-minded people. That's where networking comes in. Yes, I know networking can be tough in a new city. Where do we start? How do we find people?

The smartest way to find the "right" networking opportunity is to Google this line:

"[your city] chamber of commerce young professionals"

Odds are, you have a local chamber of commerce, which often holds networking events for business professionals.

> NOTE: Some chambers have a group designed for young professionals in their 20s and 30s.

If you find a contact person for the general networking or young professional group, send a note and ask about the next meeting/event.

Subject line: Interested in joining [name of young professional group]

Hi _____,

My name is [first and last name], and I am [new to the area/a recent grad/a young professional in the area]. It's nice to meet you.

I see the [name of city] Chamber of Commerce has a [networking group/ young professional division called _____]. I would like to learn more about the group and how I can be involved.

Please let me know what information you can provide.

Thanks so much,

– Your first and last name

Email signature

If you can't locate the right group through the chamber, then it's time for Plan B. On your local chamber website, find a staff person who works in events or communications. Those people tend to be on the "pulse" of the business community. Then, send an email like this:

Subject line: Interested in joining young professional group in [city where you live]

Hi there,

My name is _____, and I am [new to the area/a recent grad/a young professional in the area]. I am interested in networking opportunities here in town and curious if you know about anything through the chamber or in the general community.

Please feel free to connect me with the right person or people.

Thanks so much,

– Your first and last name

Email signature

More Google searches for networking opportunities:

– If you want to find a networking group for people in your industry, it's a bit trickier. That's because if you search...

"[your industry] networking [your city]"...

...you will probably see a list of job postings and not networking groups. So you'll need to use other keywords. Try these:

"[your industry] society [your city]"

"[your industry] association [your city]"

"[your industry] roundtable [your city]"

For women and ethnic/cultural groups:

"[your industry] women [your city]"

"[your industry] [your cultural or ethnic background] [your city]"

For college alumni groups:

"[your college] alumni association [your city]"

> NOTE: Don't forget to tap into online alumni networks too. You can find nearby alumni who might work at desirable companies.

QUICK TIP — The secret to a strong networking subject line

What's in a name? When it comes to networking, a heck of a lot.

The secret to a strong networking subject line? First and last names. The title of the email must contain the names of people relevant to your message.

"Friend of Roger Mullins, hope to connect over coffee"

"Co-worker of Shirley Applegate, interested in sales position"

"Keisha Summers, freelancer you met at the business roundtable"

When you use the name of the person you have in common — or reference the specific place or event where you two connected — it makes the person MUCH more likely to open your email and respond.

Suddenly, your message is not spam, random or unfamiliar. Because you prove you know people in common or already met once before, you create a level of trust.

So drop names and make the connection right away.

Relationship Building

HOW TO NETWORK WITH ALUMNI FROM YOUR SCHOOL

You know who alumni love? Other people who went to their college or university. Fellow alumni can be your biggest advocate and resource as you network and look for jobs.

Send the email, start the conversation and see where it takes you.

Subject line: [Name of college/university][student/alumnus/alumna], needs your advice

> *NOTE: Why should you admit you want "advice"? It is a non-threatening email intro. You don't ask straight up for a job. No, you want the person's wisdom.*

Hi _____,

My name is [your fist and last name], and I am a [year in school, recent grad or alumnus/alumna] from [name of college/university].

I [explain how you obtained the person's email address; for instance, "found your email address in the university's alumni database and thought I would reach out"].

I am interested in the [specific industry] field and see that's the kind of work you do. In particular, I would like to learn more about your experience with [name a specific project from the person's LinkedIn profile or company website and why you find it compelling; for instance, "the recent

73

high-rise bridge your team built in western New York. That's the kind of large-scale construction I hope to work on"]. I would also appreciate your advice as I navigate the job market.

Please let me know if you have time for a brief phone call or in-person meeting.

Thanks so much,

– Your first name

Email signature

Deeper Insight

You and an alumnus/alumna have an immediate connection — you both have fond memories of time spent on the same campus. THEN, you ask to learn from the person AND reference a highlight from his/her career. What a complimentary email!

How to connect two people who should know each other

Networking isn't all about you. Sometimes, it's the decision to connect other people so they can find success.

Be a giver. Pay it forward. The template below will show you how.

Subject line: Two people who should know each other

[First name 1], meet [First name 2].

[First name 2], meet [First name 1].

I think it's time you two are properly introduced. I realize you work in a similar space and could collaborate in the future.

[First name 1]: [First name 2] is a [explain what person #2 is all about; for instance, "John is a graphic designer who does a lot of work for nonprofits. Here's a link to some of his work"].

74

[First name 2]: [First name 1] is a [explain what person #1 is all about; for instance, "Jane is a development associate at Big Nonprofit and had mentioned she needs a new designer for upcoming projects"].

> NOTE: Links are important. Allow the two people to research each other right away.

Feel free to reply and start the conversation.

Thanks and good luck!

– Your first name

Email signature

Deeper Insight

Let each person know about the other's interests or experience. It makes the intro stronger and more meaningful.

Then, link to each person's website or work, step back and allow the two to chat.

How to ask for a conversation with a professional in your field

If you're curious about a job in your field or perhaps a new industry altogether, a conversation with the right person is a great way to find answers.

Subject line: Looking for advice about the [particular field; for instance, "environmental nonprofit"] field

Hi _____,

My name is [first and last name], and I am a [who you are in context; for instance, "recent grad from Big State University/friend of your colleague Michael Williams"]. I hope you're doing well.

I received your email from [the person who may have connected you] who thought I should reach out and introduce myself.

I want to learn more about [the particular field; for instance, "environmental nonprofits as I'm interested in the field and a potential career change"]. I see you [a tidbit from the person's company bio or LinkedIn profile; for instance, "have spent several years in the environmental nonprofit field, most recently with Big Nonprofit"]. I would appreciate your insight as I consider my next steps.

Are you available to meet for coffee over the next week?

> *NOTE: Ask for the in-person meeting and not a phone call. A physical introduction is always better if you live or work near each other. Let the other person request a phone call if necessary but don't prompt one on your own.*

Please let me know and thanks so much,

– Your first name

Email signature

Deeper Insight

Allow 48 hours for a response. If you don't receive an answer after two days, write back with, "I'm checking to make sure you saw my email from the other day. Please let me know if you're available for a brief conversation. Thanks again."

If still no response after the follow-up message, try to reach the person by phone. If you can't pin down the person by phone, it might be time to network with someone else.

How to ask a person to help you in a mentor capacity

Mentors are everywhere. We live in a hyper-connected world and no matter the question, there's bound to be someone a click away with the answer.

Between Twitter, Facebook, LinkedIn and your email contacts, you own a vast network of topic experts. The next time you need help, take five minutes and search for a friend or colleague who might be the ideal resource.

Subject line: Need your advice, [explain task at hand; for instance, "looking for job opportunities"]

Hi _____,

[If you know the person, open with a little chit chat; for instance, "How's everything going at Big State? Are your students prepping for final exams?"]

[If you don't know the person, explain who you are; for instance, "My name is _____, and I'm a graduate student at Big State University working on a master's in French literature. I came across your profile on LinkedIn and thought I'd make introductions."]

I am focused now on [the task at hand; for instance, "landing a job after graduation"] and would appreciate the chance to ask you questions. I know you have experience with [the task at hand] and can give me some pointers to stand out and make an impact.

I realize your time is valuable so please let me know what you can do.

[If the person lives near you, write, "I would be happy to come by your office or meet up for coffee."]

[If the person lives in another city or state, write, "A quick phone call would be great."]

> NOTE: Once the person meets you, either in person or over the phone, the conversation may prompt new ways he/she can connect you with others.

Thanks so much, and I hope to hear from you.

– Your first name

Email signature

Deeper Insight

In general, people like to be treated as mentors and asked for their advice. In your email, make sure the person understands why you need assistance and what you hope to accomplish. Then, allow 48 hours for a response and follow up if you receive no answer.

How to ask someone for career advice or direction

Let's say you aren't sure the direction to take your career. Then it's helpful to sit with someone you trust and explore options.

If you write someone you know:

Subject line: Career questions, could use your advice

Hi _____,

I hope everything is going well at _____.

I am at a crossroads with my career right now and could use your guidance. [Then, provide detail in one or two lines about why you need help; for instance, "I am working right now at a research lab but think I might want to go back to school for a PhD. I would value your perspective before I make any big moves."]

> NOTE: *"Value your perspective"* — *that line will make the other person feel like a million bucks.*

Please let me know if we can get together over the next week and talk for a bit.

Thanks so much,

– Your first name

Email signature

If you write someone you don't know or don't know too well:

Subject line: Career questions, could use your advice

Hi _____,

My name is _____, and I [put yourself in context and how you came upon this person; for instance, "found your name in the alumni directory for Big State University"]. I hope you're doing well.

I am at a crossroads with my career right now and could use your guidance. [Then explain in one to two lines why you need help; for instance, "I am working right now at a research lab but think I might want to go back to school for a PhD. I would value your perspective before I make any big moves."]

[Then, since the person is a relative stranger, explain why you would "value" the person's perspective; for instance, "As someone who went through the PhD program, I hope you can help me understand the pros and cons of the decision."]

Please let me know if we can get together over the next week and talk for a bit.

Thanks so much,

– Your first name

Email signature

Deeper Insight

With the "career advice" email, it's important to seek someone's good counsel and not ask for a job. The email also allows you to begin a *conversation*. And — who knows? — maybe your inquisitiveness *leads* to a job.

Here are more subject lines you can use or adapt.

General networking:

Friend of [mutual acquaintance] who needs your advice

Fellow [your industry] professional who needs your advice

To college alumni:

Fellow [your college/university] grad looking for advice

Someone notable you admire:

Big fan of your work looking for advice

Interoffice:

New employee who needs your advice

How to ask someone you respect to review your work

Even the greatest writers have editors. If you have an important document, project or presentation, ask someone who has a keen eye to look it over or even chop it up in Microsoft Word via Track Changes.

Subject line: Would appreciate your review of my [project at hand]

Hi _____,

> NOTE: Your tone will vary if you write to a friend or someone you've
> never met. Use the appropriate version below based on the nature
> of your relationship.

Formal introduction

My name is [first and last name], and I am a [who you are in context; for
instance, "graduate student at _____, aspiring writer or amateur
photographer"]. It's nice to meet you.

[Explain how and why you respect the other person; for instance, "I'm a
huge fan of your mystery novels and love the work you do." Then, go one
layer deeper and give the person an example of why you like his/her work;
for instance, "Your latest book, *Title of the Book,* is such a terrific read,
and you do a great job explaining the origins of the American highway
system. Such a fascinating story."]

Informal introduction

[If you know the person already, open with a little small talk like, "How's
the life of a novelist these days? Got any big projects in the works?"]

The rest of the email — both versions

[Now get to the "ask"; for instance, "I wrote a short story called _____,
and I would love your opinion on my style and how the story flows." Then,
explain what you hope to accomplish; for instance, "I am working hard to
develop my voice as a short story writer and know I will improve much
faster if people I respect give me pointers."]

[To conclude, respect the person's time; for instance, "I know your time
is valuable, and I appreciate any help you can offer."]

Thanks so much,

– Your first name

Email signature

Deeper Insight

You must give before you can get. Praise the other person and also explain how you need that person's critiques because he/she will make your work better.

At the end, recognize the person's time is valuable and be thankful no matter how much — or how little — the person chooses to help.

How to make someone aware of you as a subject matter expert

Are you a subject-matter expert or SME? Of course you are.

Think about what you know well. Maybe it's running, healthy eating, commercial real estate…whatever it is, you should leverage your knowledge online to generate momentum for your career.

The best way to become a SME is to introduce yourself to the people who run relevant blogs and websites.

Subject line: Making introductions, resource on [your area of expertise; for instance, "commercial real estate"]

Hi [first name of the person who runs the blog or website],

My name is [first and last name], and I am a [job title and your company if you're in a job]. I hope you're doing well.

I'm writing to introduce myself and make you aware of me as a resource for [your particular topic; for instance, "trends in commercial real estate"].

I have a lot of respect for [name of blog/website/publication] and would like to contribute in a way that's meaningful for your audience. Your recent article called [article title; for instance, "The Future of the Philly Exurbs"] is insightful and the kind of information people need today.

> NOTE: Provide the actual title of the article you find notable and link to it. Don't write "I think your website is great." Take the time to show you're serious.

[Now give the person two or three sentences on what makes you an SME. Something like…

"I work here in Philadelphia at Acme Corporation and often write about real estate trends on our company blog. Two quick examples: Name of Column 1 and Name of Column 2.

I have also spoken to business groups including the Big Trade Association and the Little Trade Association about trends in the real estate market."]

Please let me know if I can ever provide a quote for an article or analysis on future real estate topics. I am also available to help with any workshops/ seminars and can send over guest posts.

> NOTE: Tell the person you're flexible: you can be quoted as an expert, lead a workshop or write a guest post. Whatever the person needs, you're game.

Thanks, and I hope to hear from you.

– Your first name

Email signature

___

Deeper Insight

The pitch email above has two goals: make the initial introduction and explain why you're a worthy SME.

You need to stroke the ego and tell the person why you admire the website/blog/ publication. Then, go into detail on your expertise in the field and include specific examples and links.

Hopefully, the SME email pitch will elicit a nice response and, above all, begin a relationship that could propel your career in all kinds of ways.

How to ask if you can guest post on a blog or website

Let's talk about guest posts, an excellent strategy to grow a personal website or brand. Guest posts on larger sites can send traffic back to your blog and introduce your writing to new audiences.

I have done my fair share of "guest post" email pitches and know the introductory email must strike the right tone. In my experience, there are two critical pieces:

1. Compliment the blog/website where you want to guest post.
2. Link the reader to two or three examples of your work.

So…the template:

Subject line: Interest in writing a guest post for [name of blog/website]

Hi [first name of the person who runs the site],

My name is [first and last name], and I write the blog _____, [one line about your website and why it matters; for instance, "ABC Careers, which provides career advice to young professionals"]. I hope you're doing well.

I am a big fan of [site where you want to guest post] and read your content all the time. I especially like [link to two recent posts you find worthwhile;

for instance, "your post called <u>Name of Post 1</u> and one called <u>Name of Post 2</u>"].

[Then, one more compliment that leads into your pitch; for instance, "I like your site because the advice is practical, and I have similar content I think your audience would appreciate."]

> NOTE: Most people don't link to articles from the site where they want to contribute. Fewer still explain WHY they enjoy the posts they reference.

I wrote a blog post recently called [blog post title that's linked to the post], and in a nutshell it's about [quick line on what the post is about; for instance, "smart tips for dealing with rude co-workers"]. I would be happy to send it over as a guest post if you'd like. Here are a couple other recent posts I've done:

– [blog post title that's linked to the post]

– [blog post title that's linked to the post]

If you have other ideas, I am open to writing something else for [the site where you want to guest post].

> NOTE: What you're "saying" is...I will play by your rules so tell me what you want. I am the guest poster and don't call the shots.

Thanks, and I hope to hear from you.

– Your first name

Email signature

Deeper Insight

First, praise the other person and mention how much you enjoy his/her website by linking to recent content. That's a nice ego boost for the site manager and goes a long way.

Then, link to your own content and give the person a few guest post options. You also mention you're happy to write something else entirely if that's what the person wants.

How to thank the person for allowing you to guest post

Once your guest post appears, you need to then thank the editor or publisher for the chance to contribute. Ideally, you'll want to offer more guest posts so now is the chance to solidify the relationship and become a go-to writer for the blog or website.

Subject line: Thank you for running my [article/column/guest post]

Hi [first name of the person who runs the site],

Thank you again for publishing my [article/column/guest post] called [name of post with the link included]. I think the [article/column/guest post] turned out great, and I appreciate the chance to appear on [name of website where you contributed].

I will be sure to share the post on my social media channels today and throughout the week. On occasion, can I send you other pieces I write? I'd like to contribute again if that's possible.

> NOTE: Not only did you provide content to fill out the person's website, but you're also willing to share the piece on social media. That's a double dose of helpful, and the person will make special note of it.

86

Please let me know and have a great day,

– Your first name

Email signature

Deeper Insight

You should always thank the publisher/editor who runs your work. That's a smart way to build on your budding relationship.

Finally, offer to submit your work again. Most website editors need fresh content day after day. If the editor can rely on you for new articles or columns, you could find yourself as a regular contributor.

QUICK TIP — Six most powerful words in networking

Once you secure a networking meeting, you need to ask smart questions. The best way? Learn to love **WHO, WHAT, WHEN, WHERE, WHY** and **HOW**.

These six words demonstrate maturity, selflessness and a natural curiosity. They prove you can be genuinely interested in another person's life. And perhaps through all your questions, you'll find new ways to connect or advance your career.

"Curiosity is more important than knowledge." — *Albert Einstein*

WHO should I talk to like this?

Anyone. A stranger at a happy hour, someone you've asked to meet for coffee or even a random person you sit next to on a plane. Everyone else knows something you don't. Listening is key.

Sample question: Who are some of your clients?

WHAT do I talk about?

Talk about what the other person wants to talk about. Let him/her guide the conversation. If he says, "I like my job, but it can be tough at times," then you come right back with, "What makes it tough?"

Sample question: What kind of projects are you working on?

WHEN is the most appropriate time?

Anytime. People love to talk about themselves. In fact, they'll probably give you as much info as you can handle. They think, "You're curious about what I do for a living? Of course I'll blab about it!"

Sample question: When did you decide to focus on that aspect of your career?

WHERE are the best places?

Anywhere, but specifically situations where you could aid your career. Networking events, work conferences and job interviews are great places to give the "six words" a try.

Sample question: Where do you go most often for work? Do you travel?

WHY is it such an effective strategy?

With each question, you take the conversation deeper and build trust. Plus, if you two find a way to network further, the person is more likely to help because he likes you — and all you did was let him ramble on about himself!

Sample question: Why did you decide to pursue a master's degree?

HOW do I keep up with all the questions?

You listen intently. You stay in the moment, absorb what the person has to say and come back with a thoughtful response.

Sample question: How did you start your own business? What was the process?

————

In conversation, our instinct is to cut in and say, "Well, I…"

But you…you're smarter than that. You understand the power of **WHO, WHAT, WHEN, WHERE, WHY** and **HOW.**

Those six words allow you to forge relationships, broaden your knowledge and create new career opportunities.

"Why?"

When you focus on others, the world starts to shift in your favor.

Tricky Situations

HOW TO RESPOND TO AN AWKWARD EMAIL

People send unpredictable work-related emails all the time.

The upside of strange messages? You have the opportunity to send a composed, professional response.

Let's explore one awkward scenario, understand how to reply and then discuss broader lessons.

Example: You write someone who might be able to connect you with a company that's hiring. The person responds and says, "Sure, I'm happy to help. Also, could I have a few minutes of your time to discuss an online learning course my company offers? I think you'd benefit as you look for work."

Whoa there. You asked for a connection to a job. Now the guy wants to sell you something.

That's pretty awkward.

So what do you say?

"Thanks for connecting me to your friend and helping with my job search. You can use my current email address, and here are a few highlights from my resume so you can write a strong intro:

- Highlight 1
- Highlight 2
- Highlight 3

As for your request about online courses, you can send over the information and I'm happy to take a look.

Thanks again for the help."

Let's break down the response. First, the person stays focused and gives the helper enough info to write a strong networking email.

Then, to deal with the awkward part, the person politely asks to receive the information about the online course and make a decision at a later date. That's a nice enough answer to ensure the networking email happens and the person feels you valued his/her product.

To bring it all together…

Awkward situations require you to be:

– Cordial

– Patient

– Diplomatic

Don't shut people out or fire back with a rude response.

If you must say "No" to an odd request, let the person down gently. If you don't need to say "No" in the moment, leave the door open a crack so the person feels validated.

Awkward email conversations are everywhere. What counts the most is how you handle them and manage your own reputation.

How to tell people you changed jobs

When you change jobs, it's often helpful to update your professional network. Otherwise, people find out when they email your old work address and it bounces back with, "I no longer work here. Please contact _____ instead."

Also, if everyone knows you switched jobs, you open yourself up to new opportunities and ways to connect. A friend might respond with, "Hey, I didn't know you work at _____ now. Let's grab coffee and see if our teams could ever collaborate."

Be your own PR machine.

Subject line: Career update — I changed jobs

Hi everyone,

Hope you're doing well.

[This week/this month], I began a new job at [name of company, link to the company and then an explanation of what the company does; for instance,

"Acme Corporation, a leader in industrial supplies and tools"]. I will be a [job title] and focus on [the primary role at the job; for instance, "sales in the greater Milwaukee region"].

> *NOTE: People will want to learn about your new company. Provide a link to make it easy.*

[If you need to explain why you left your most recent job, don't dwell on the negative. Remember, your extended network will see the email so you should convey a sense of confidence. You could include a line like, "While I enjoyed my time at _____, I'm excited about my new opportunity and think it's a great time to make the move."]

My new email is [email address] and office phone is [phone number]. If there are any ways we could work together, please let me know. I'm happy to grab coffee and explore opportunities.

Thanks, and feel free to reply and update me on your career.

> *NOTE: Show you're also interested in your friends' careers. Maybe someone else recently changed jobs? It's never only about you.*

Have a great day,

– Your first name

New work email signature

Deeper Insight

In the email, be direct, include relevant contact info and beam with positivity about the career change. Plus, invite people to write back so you know the latest on their careers. In one email, you cover all your bases.

How to follow up if someone said he/she would pass along your resume

Someone offers to send your resume to the right person at a company. Then a few days go by, and you're not sure if the resume went anywhere. Now it's time to check back and stay in pursuit of the job.

Subject line: Checking in, resume help for [your first and last name]

Hi _____,

I hope you're doing well.

I am _____, and I [remind the person how you two became acquainted]. [Earlier this week/last week] you mentioned you could pass along my resume to [the person who you want to see it]. It would be great if you're still able to do that.

If so, please remind [the person] [one or two lines on why you are the best candidate for the position; give your networker a bit of ammo he/she can use. For instance, "I recently finished a year-long program teaching English in China and understand how to manage a classroom of young children"].

> NOTE: Never assume people remember you or what you need from them.

Again, I appreciate your willingness to help me.

Please let me know if you have any questions.

Thanks,

– Your first name

Email signature

Deeper Insight

Be polite but confident. You need the resume to find its way to the right person so you shouldn't hesitate with the follow-up email. Fight for your career.

How to ask for a reply if a person doesn't answer in a timely manner

You send an email and need a response ASAP. And then you wait. And wait. You begin to wonder if your original email ever went through. It's time to check back in.

Also, the subject line should remind the person why you're following up. So in the part labeled "the reason," give a quick description. For instance, "Following up, renovation proposal."

Subject line: Following up, [the reason; for instance, "renovation proposal"]

Hi Mr./Ms. _____, [if the email is to an employer or someone you don't know]

Hi _____, [first-name basis if the email is to someone you know]

Good morning/afternoon.

I am following up on the [reason you need to hear from the person; for instance, "status of your proposal for the renovations to the shopping mall"].

> NOTE: I typically avoid "-ing" words ("following"), but in this case it makes sense.

Please let me know when you plan to send over the information. I am available if you have any questions.

Thanks,

– Your first and last name

Email signature

Deeper Insight

Be courteous, not pushy. Even if you desperately need the other person to respond, play it cool.

How to write a friend of a friend about a potential job opening

If you reach out to a person you only know through someone else, you must be a clear communicator.

For starters, the subject line should include who you are in relation to the person you write. For instance, "Friend of Dave Wilson, [name of company] job opening."

Subject line: Friend of _____, [name of company] job opening

Hi _____, [first-name basis since it's a friend of a friend]

My name is _____, and I am a friend of [the friend who connects the two of you]. I hope you're doing well.

I am a [recent grad from _____ or list your job title] and noticed a position on the [name of company] website I believe is a good fit for me. I [explain in one sentence why you're a "good fit." For instance, "spent the past three years doing a similar job as a branch manager for Acme Corporation"].

Can you give me any insight into the hiring process? Also, are you able to pass my resume to the right person at the company?

> NOTE: Don't send your resume yet. If the person responds, then pass it along. Don't be too forward or aggressive.

Please let me know what's possible and if you need me to send along additional info. I appreciate any help you can offer.

Thanks,

– Your first and last name

Email signature

Deeper Insight

Hopefully, the fact that you have a common connection (a mutual friend) will encourage the person to help. Be confident, explain yourself clearly and always be gracious for the assist.

How to ask someone to make an introduction on your behalf

Referrals are pure gold in networking and the job market. To maximize the opportunity, arm the person who will make the introduction with highlights from your bio.

Subject line: Introducing me to [the person you want to meet]

Hi _____,

Hope you're doing well. [If you're friendly enough, add in something like, "How's the dissertation coming along? I know those can be a total grind."]

If you need a job:

I am in the job market and want to meet key people in the [specific industry] space. In particular, I would like to connect with [the person you want to meet]. Would you be willing to send an email and introduce me? If so, here are three quick bullets [the person you want to meet] might find interesting.

- [Three facts about your skills or experience relevant to the job and the person in question. For instance, "1. Proficient at Software Tool 1, Software Tool 2 and Software Tool 3."]

I have also attached my resume if you'd like to include it in your email.

NOTE: Don't make the person respond with, "Can you send me your resume?" Send it over the first time.

95

Please let me know what you can do and if you need me to provide any other information.

Thanks so much,

– Your first name

Email signature

If you want to make a business connection:

As I grow my business, I hope to meet key people in the [specific industry] space. In particular, I want to connect with [the person you want to meet]. Would you be willing to send an email and introduce me? If so, here are three quick bullets [the person you want to meet] might find interesting.

[Three facts about your business; use data, hard numbers and specific details. For instance, "Our company is the fastest-growing solar panel distributor in the US, and business grew 240 percent in the past year."]

> *NOTE: Use your work experience to demonstrate results and how you're the kind of person who "gets stuff done."*

Please let me know what you can do and if I need to provide any other information.

Thanks so much,

– Your first name

Email signature

Deeper Insight

Whether you need a job or want to network for business, it's important to provide your friend with info to bolster the "introduction" email he/she will write.

How to network during the busy holiday season

Holiday season means everyone is away from their desks on vacation, right? Maybe. Maybe not.

If you send a networking email the right way, it doesn't matter if the person is tied up or free to chat.

Subject line: Looking to connect

Hi _____,

I hope you had a great [Thanksgiving/Christmas/holiday] break.

I know [November/December] is a busy time of year, but if possible I would like to get together and talk about [the task at hand; for instance, "new ways our companies can work together in the coming year"].

> NOTE: "busy time of year" — recognize you might catch the person at a hectic moment.

Please let me know a day/time that works for you.

Thanks so much,

– Your first name

Email signature

Deeper Insight

The most important part of the email is to recognize the holiday season is go-go-go ("I know December is a busy time of year…"). Then you allow the other person to write, "Sorry, December is bad for me. How about January?"

Or the person could write, "Sure, I can find time for a meeting. How about December 15 at 2 p.m.?"

Then you land an important face-to-face conversation to set you up for the year ahead.

OK. Let's say the person doesn't answer your email. Ever.

What then? Do you write a follow up a few days later? Do you leave it alone until after the New Year?

Again, you can check back in as long as you understand the person might be busy. Wait two or three days and then send a note like this:

Hi _____,

I am following up on the email I sent a few days ago about meeting this month. I know you might be busy with the holidays, but when you have a chance please let me know if you're free.

Thanks,

– Your first name

Deeper Insight

The follow-up message keeps your foot on the gas but shows you understand the person might be incommunicado.

How to fill out "Contact Us" boxes

"Contact Us" forms are the worst, right?

The empty squares are so limiting. We can't link to any URLs, and the entire message feels impersonal. How can we stand out in a box designed to rein us in?

Here's a template if, for example, you write a company to explain your own company's services.

Name: Derrick Matthews

Email: XXXX@_____.com

Website: XXXX

Your message:

Hi there,

I'm Derrick Matthews, a regional sales rep for Acme Corporation (http://www._____.com), North Carolina's largest medical device supplier.

I'll be in the Greensboro area next week and would like to stop by your practice, introduce myself and explain the products and services we offer. I researched [name of company's] website and think there are ways we can work together. In particular, [an update or project from the website that stands out to you; for instance, "I see you recently hired Dr. Zeke Ozkowski, who specializes in infant heart defects. We have a new line of cardiology equipment he might find valuable"].

We have competitive prices and fast turnaround times on all orders. To see testimonials about our service, click here: http://bit.ly/XXXX. For our client list, go here: http://bit.ly/XXXX.

NOTE: Consider a link shortener like bit.ly so you don't paste giant links and take up space.

Thanks, and I hope to hear from you soon.

– Derrick Matthews
Regional Sales Rep, Acme Corporation
Email: XXXX@_____.com
Office: XXX-XXX-XXXX Cell: XXX-XXX-XXXX

Deeper Insight

Keep the message brief in the "Contact Us" box. It's possible the message becomes one giant, messy blob when the person receives it — like everything is one long paragraph, even the intro line "Hi there." So the shorter the better.

Also reference the other person's company or website. We're accustomed to think every random message via a "Contact Us" form is spam or the exact same email sent to 1,000 other websites. Make yours unique and catch the reader by surprise — in a good way.

Finally, include your email signature even though you already provided contact info in the form boxes.

QUICK TIP — Follow up if you don't receive a response

Despite your best efforts and perfect networking emails, the person might not respond the first time.

Maybe the person is too busy to answer or never saw your email. Either way, you have the right to check back in and stay in pursuit.

In most cases, give the person 48 hours to respond. If there's still no answer, reply to the email you first sent over and write:

Hi _____,

Please let me know if you saw my email from [the day you sent it]. If possible, I would like [what you want from the person; for instance, "to grab coffee and pick your brain about applying to law school"].

Thanks, and I hope to hear from you.

– Your first name

Deeper Insight

If the person doesn't answer the second time, make sure you have the email address correct. Also check if the person has another email address (ex: some people read work email all the time but personal email sporadically).

If you REALLY want to network with the person, try a third email a week after the second one. If you don't receive an answer after the third try, you may need to walk away and message someone else.

Thank-You Notes

HOW TO THANK A CO-WORKER OR CLIENT WHO WENT ABOVE AND BEYOND

Thank-you notes are the easiest way to stand out and strengthen a relationship. The templates I provide take only a few minutes to write, but their impact lasts much, much longer.

Find a spare moment in the day and send off a thank-you note. Your *career* will thank you too.

> NOTE: If you have the time and it feels appropriate, send a handwritten note instead. It will mean more than an email — although a thank-you email is still nice.

Subject line: Thank you again for [how the person helped you; for instance, "help on the financial report"]

Hi [first name],

Thank you so much for the help recently. [Then, be specific and let the person know exactly how he/she helped; for instance, "The year-end financial report was a huge task, and it was great to have your knowledge and assistance to finish the job."]

Please let me know how I can help with your own projects. I'm more than happy to lend a hand.

> NOTE: Always offer to return the favor.

Thanks again and have a great day,

– Your first name

Email signature

Deeper Insight

Reference exactly how the person helped you. The details take the email from a "quick little thank you" to a "this meant a lot to me." The person will recognize the extra effort.

How to thank someone for connecting you to another person

Subject line: Thank you again for the connection

Hi [first name],

Thank you so much for the recent help with [my job search/my business/ however else the person lent a hand]. [Then, be specific and let the person know how he/she gave you a boost; for instance, "Since you introduced me to Tom Roush, I have started to freelance at his magazine and love the work I'm doing. Here's my latest article on the rise of local craft breweries."]

I'm grateful for your assistance and how you made Tom aware of me.

Please let me know how I can help with your own career. I'm more than happy to lend a hand.

NOTE: Always offer to return the favor.

102

Thanks again and have a great day,

– Your first name

Email signature

Deeper Insight

If applicable, it's nice to show the person an example of the work you do now thanks to the connection. Then you prove once more how much the person has done for you.

How to thank an employee at an internship or a new job

Subject line: Thank you for all the help

Hi _____,

Thank you for all your help the past few weeks [at my internship/as I adjusted to the new job]. It was great to have someone who could answer questions and introduce me to people. I [reference a specific moment in which the person helped you; for instance, "would have been lost in that first meeting when we had to update the team on our progress. You bailed me out there"].

Thanks again,

– Your first name

Email signature

Deeper Insight

It takes 30 seconds to make someone's day. You also strengthen the relationship with the person who mentored you. Remember: you need allies as you grow within an organization and make your name.

How to thank someone for a referral that led to a business deal

---

Subject line: Thank you again for the referral [or business connection]

Hi _____,

Thank you so much for [referring my name/passing my name] to [name of person] at [company where you landed a deal]. This week, I found out our company secured the [business/contract/deal].

> NOTE: Include the company and name of the person involved in the business deal. Don't make your friend rack his/her brain to remember the fine details of the situation.

I am thrilled to work with [name of company] and forever grateful you helped to make it happen. If I can return the favor in any way, please ask.

Have a great day,

– Your first name

Email signature

Deeper Insight

The person should know if his/her networking led you to a successful venture. You should always take 30 seconds and give a recap. The person who assisted you will feel great for days — even though you picked up the business for your own company.

How to thank someone for a referral that led to a new job

Subject line: Got the job, thanks for all your help

Hi _____,

Thank you so much for [referring my name/passing my name] for the [job title] position at [name of company]. This week, I found out I landed the job!

> NOTE: The above sentence is one example where I allow an exclamation mark in an email. Good news deserves an exclamation. More on "!" on page 45.

I am excited to start at [name of company] and forever grateful you helped to make it happen. If I can return the favor in any way, please ask.

Have a great day,

– Your first name

Email signature

Deeper Insight

As a practical matter, the person should know if his/her networking helped you with the job. Plus, you should always thank people who play a pivotal role in your career. It is common courtesy and a fundamental of networking.

QUICK TIP — The "I can email you my questions" strategy

Networking is all about relationships.

The gold medal: schedule a face-to-face conversation, shake hands and talk in person.

The silver medal: schedule a video chat or phone call and meet each other — albeit in separate rooms.

There's a bronze medal, but you don't want to wear it around your neck. That's when you offer to email someone a list of questions in case he/she is too busy to talk with you.

Then the end of the networking email looks like this:

Please let me know if you have time to meet in person or talk by phone. If it's easier, I can send over a list of questions.

Yes, it *would* be easier for the person to knock out answers to your questions, send them back and be done with you. But then, where's the relationship? Did you two ever meet and build trust and camaraderie? Not really.

Don't let the person out of an actual conversation. If you ask for advice in a genuine way, as I explain in many of the networking email templates, you make it tough for the person to brush you off.

You need new relationships and connections. You need gold and silver.

Pretend as if bronze doesn't exist.

Chapter 4
Job Search Templates

Job Search Overview

As you explore job opportunities, keep this sentence in mind:

"I must provide detail at every turn."

Assume no one knows anything about you — even a friend, colleague or boss — when you describe yourself and your work experience in emails and job applications.

In an email introduction, you're not a "recent grad from the Big State University who also interned at an environmental research firm."

No, you're a "recent sociology grad from Big State University who also interned for the past 11 months at the Big Nonprofit chapter here in Connecticut."

The stuff that counts: sociology, 11 months, Big Nonprofit.

It doesn't even matter if you apply for a job AT the Big Nonprofit. You should still tell people you interned there and for how long. Never gloss over the details. They distinguish you from the other job applicants and ensure employers never have to ask a question like:

"Hmmm, what environmental research firm used her as an intern? I wish she had told me."

QUICK TIP — "TEN COMMANDMENTS" OF JOB SEARCH EMAILS

Let us proclaim from the mountain these ten rules for job search emails.

I. Be cordial — "I hope you're doing well."

II. Be aware — "I will be brief because I know you're busy."

III. Be inquisitive — "I checked out your company website and respect your mission to teach music in schools. Do you plan to expand to more schools this year?"

IV. Be descriptive — "I'm a friend of Shanice Richards, who told me to write an email and introduce myself."

V. Be thankful — "I appreciate any help you can provide."

VI. Be straightforward — "I'm writing to see if I can visit the office for an informational interview."

VII. Be concise — No giant paragraphs.

VIII. Be patient — Give people 24–48 hours to respond before the follow up.

IX. Be cautious — No spelling or grammar mistakes; first impressions are huge.

X. Be brave — Press "Send" and let the chips fall where they may.

How to apply for a job and attach a resume/cover letter

WE ALL KNOW THE DRILL. APPLY FOR A JOB WITH AN INTRODUCTORY EMAIL AND ATTACH YOUR RESUME/COVER LETTER.

How do we stand out to ensure the person looks at our application?

If you're able to send an email (rather than apply through a website), tease your career highlights in the email body.

Subject line: [First and last name], applying for the position of _____

> NOTE: Include your first and last name as well as the position you
> want. Make it easy on the person who receives your information.

Hi [name of person who should receive the application; if you don't know a name, write "Dear Hiring Professional"],

> NOTE: For the proper way to address the employer, go to page 27.

My name is [first and last name] and I am applying for the position of [job title] at [name of company]. I have attached my cover letter and resume to this email.

You'll notice my cover letter tells a short story about how I [tease the cover letter and make the reader want to check it out; for instance, "uploaded an entire donor database in a weekend to ensure the organization was ready for a big pledge drive the following Monday"].

> NOTE: For more on how to write a "storytelling" cover letter, see
> page 195.

Thanks, and please let me know if you have any questions.

– Your first name

Email signature

Deeper Insight

I know it's "outside the box" to tease your cover letter here, but if you don't, the email won't stand out.

It's time to break the mold.

How to apply for a job at the same place where you've been turned down

A company rejected you once. So what? If you gained new skills and experience and feel you're a more qualified candidate the second time around, go for the job.

Subject line: [First and last name], applying for the position of _____

Hi _____,

My name is [first and last name] and I am applying for the position of [job title] at [name of company]. You might recognize my name because in [month of year; for instance, "December of 2012"] I applied for the position of [job title].

> NOTE: Right away, explain you're the same person who applied for another job at the same company. Don't make people wonder, "Wait, is this the same guy from before?"

Since then, I have gained new skills and believe I am a great fit for the [job title] position.

Please see my attached cover letter and resume. You'll notice my cover letter tells a short story about how I [tease the cover letter and make the reader want to check it out; for instance, "overcame my toughest day at Acme Corporation and still came through for the client"].

Thanks so much, and let me know if I can provide additional information.

– Your first name

Email signature

Deeper Insight

The "storytelling" cover letter tease will make the employer think, "OK, now I have to see what this person is all about."

Above all, you must keep the focus on you and not the other 100 applicants.

How to ask about internships or an internship application

Employers don't expect college students and other prospective interns to send strong introductory emails. That's why you can impress people right away with the template below.

Subject line: Interested in an internship at [name of company/ organization]

Hi _____,

My name is [first and last name], and I am a [freshman, sophomore, etc... at _____]. I hope you're doing well.

I see [name of company/organization] offers internships, and I want to learn more about the application process.

I am interested in [particular field; for instance, "urban planning"] and hope to gain skills and real-world experience with your team. [Give one sentence on why you like what the company does; for instance, "I researched your website and read all about your plans for Acme Apartment Complex. The project looks fantastic, and I would love to observe and be part of the planning process."]

A bit more about me: [provide two to three more details that make you look appealing; for instance, "I am on the Big State University volleyball team, a peer mentor and also the president of my dorm"]. I am a hard worker, dependable and happy to help [name of company/organization] any way I can as an intern.

111

NOTE: Give the reader your pertinent details (college, graduation year and the kind of activities you're involved in). Also let the reader know you researched the company's website and understand what the business is all about.

I have attached my resume to this email. Please let me know if I can provide any more information.

Thanks so much, and I hope to hear from you.

– Your first name

Email signature

Deeper Insight

Details, details, details. Don't send a quick note with something like, "I want to be your next intern. Here's my resume. Please let me know. Thanks!"

An email like the template above will impress even the most jaded intern coordinator.

How to ask about job opportunities as a recent grad

As you come out of school and approach employers, you need an email to prove your maturity and poise. I have seen too many email pitches from recent grads fall flat. Too much focus on "I'm a hard worker" and "I'm detail oriented." Forget that stuff.

Focus on what you have ACCOMPLISHED. Show your value.

Subject line: Interested in job opportunity at [name of company/ organization]

Hi _____,

My name is [first and last name], and I am a [senior/recent graduate at/ from _____]. I hope you're doing well.

I'm interested in a job in the [name of industry; for instance, "banking"] field and would like to learn more about [name of company/organization]. I read through [company name's] website and respect your efforts, in particular [name two and link to them; for instance, "the initiatives to teach money management in elementary schools and educate young adults on the proper use of credit. Those are innovative programs, and it seems like they make an impact"].

As a student at Big State University, I developed my [name of industry; for instance, "finance"] skills when [how you honed your ability to work in the field; for instance, "I was treasurer of my junior class and served as a TA for a freshman course called Introduction to Financial Basics"].

Here are a few more examples of my work:

– [link to examples, if available; you can also attach files if it makes more sense]

– Example #2

– Example #3

> NOTE: Examples you can share: blog posts about your work in the particular field, articles that show your efforts or accomplishments and photos of events or activities in the industry. The "examples" section is why you need a blog or online portfolio to chronicle

your work — you will need to demonstrate success in an email to employers.

I have attached my resume to this email. Please let me know if I can provide any more information.

Thanks so much, and I hope to hear from you.

– Your first name

Email signature

Deeper Insight

With an intro email, employers need to know you researched the company and also understand what you have started, built, created, led or organized.

How to apply even if the company has no openings at the time

Typically, you apply for the positions you find on job boards and company websites. What if you discover a company you love but find it's not hiring — or at least not hiring a position relevant to your skills?

Do the unusual: apply even when there are no open positions.

Subject line: ["Recent graduate from _____" or your job title; for instance, "Fundraising specialist"] interested in career opportunities

Hi _____,

My name is [first and last name], and I am a [recent grad from _____ or job title and your expertise; for instance, a "fundraising specialist who has experience with small to medium-sized nonprofits"]. I hope you're doing well.

I realize you don't have a job posting for a [job title; for instance, "development associate"], but I would still like to make introductions and explore ways I can help your team on [however you can add value; for instance, "upcoming engagements with nonprofits"].

I checked out the [name of company] website and respect the work you do, in particular [name two; for instance, "the 10K walk to support research on brain cancer and the capital campaign to aid the river clean-up. The two projects were well orchestrated, and it's clear your team knows how to deliver results"].

> NOTE: If you want the people at the company to respect you right away, prove you thoroughly researched the work they do.

For the past _____ years, I have worked with [talk about your experience so far and list examples of past clients; for instance, "nonprofits in Minneapolis on a variety of initiatives. For example, I have fundraised for the Big Nonprofit Association and the Little Nonprofit Association"].

Please see a few examples of my work down below:

– [link to examples of your work, if available; you can also attach files if it makes more sense]

– Example #2

– Example #3

> NOTE: If you are a recent grad with no real-world experience, provide links to college projects, case studies, internships or volunteer

efforts. Also, this is why you need a blog or online portfolio — to show employers examples of your work.

I have attached my resume to this email. Please let me know if I can provide more information.

Thanks so much,

– Your first name

Email signature

Deeper Insight

So what if the company has not posted a job relevant to you or your skills? Make a smart introduction anyway and open yourself to new opportunities.

In the template, prove you researched the company, link the reader to your own projects, attach your resume and ask nicely for a reply. Then, step back and see what kind of response you receive.

How to email a friend/acquaintance at the company before an interview

As you interview for a job, it's always a plus to obtain the "inside scoop." You want the truth on the company, its culture and what to expect during an interview. To glean the knowledge, use the template below.

If you know the person well:

Subject line: Applied for [job title; for instance, "staff accountant"] at [name of company]

Hi _____,

Hope all is well!

This week, I applied for the [job title] position at [name of company]. I like what [name of company] is all about and feel I would be a great fit.

To remind you:

Include two to three quick bullets about your experience or qualifications.

- [ex: I have worked for the past two years as an accountant at Acme Hospital System]

- [ex: I specialize in account reconciliation, budgeting and preparing audit reports]

> *NOTE: Provide concrete info about your career so far. Even if you're a recent grad, reference specific experience from college or internships. Instead of "I have done a lot of accounting work lately," use actual skills (ex: "preparing audit reports") so you look more competent.*

I have a couple of questions for you:

1. Can you give me any insight into the job and the company?
2. Can you put in a word with someone involved in the hiring process?

I attached my resume to this email. Let me know if I should give you any more info.

Thanks a lot for the help,

– Your first name

Email signature

Deeper Insight

Give your friend two ways to lend a hand. Yes, of course you want your friend to go right to the HR department and say, "Hire this person. She's awesome." But that might be too pushy. Instead, ask if your friend has any insight into the hiring process. Then you give your friend a way to help even if he/she can't talk you up directly.

Finally, always assume your friend could forward your email to someone important. So even if your friend knows about your career, give extra info in case the email travels.

If the person is an acquaintance:

Subject line: Question for you, applied for [job title] at [name of company]

Hi _____,

I'm [first and last name], and [the way you know the person; for instance, "we met a couple months ago at the chamber of commerce happy hour"].

NOTE: You must explain how you know the person.

I hope you're doing well.

This week, I applied for the [job title] position at [name of company]. I like [name of company's] mission and feel I would be a great fit.

To give you a quick recap on my resume:

Include two to three quick bullets about your experience or qualifications.

- [ex: I have worked for the past two years as an accountant at Acme Hospital System]

- [ex: I specialize in account reconciliation, budgeting and preparing audit reports]

118

NOTE: Include detailed information on your background in case the acquaintance forwards along your email.

Can you provide any insight into the job and the company? I would like to know more about company culture and also how the hiring process works.

I attached my resume to this email. Please let me know if I should give you any more info.

Thanks a lot for the help,

– Your first name

Email signature

Deeper Insight

Since the person may not know you well, don't immediately ask for a recommendation to the hiring manager. Instead, engage the person in a conversation on the company and show your high level of interest. Perhaps after a few back-and-forth emails, you could build up enough trust for a personal recommendation. Either way, you will gain valuable insight into the company.

How to thank someone after a job interview

You may have nailed the job interview, and the employer is ready to offer you the job. Then…you don't send a thank-you email. Then…the employer begins to wonder, "Hmm, maybe he's not so sharp after all."

Never let doubt creep into the employer's brain. Send a proper thank-you note the same day of the interview so you continue to shine.

NOTE: If you're traveling and can't send a note the same day, it's OK to write one the next day.

Subject line: Thanks again for your time

Hi _____,

Thanks again for meeting with me this [morning/afternoon]. I appreciate your time and enjoyed learning more about the company.

[Then a line from your conversation; for instance, "The market is slow right now, but you're right to think it will come back around next year." Or a way you think you can contribute; for instance, "As we discussed, I'm interested in the position and feel my design skills would be a nice complement to your graphics department."]

> NOTE: Don't write anything which might imply you're ready to accept the position. You don't have the job yet.

If you have any further questions, please feel free to ask.

Thanks so much, and…

Two options here:

1. *Make a quick reference again to the conversation. Something like, "Thanks so much, and I hope you enjoy your weekend at the beach."*

2. *Keep it straightforward if you don't feel comfortable being "chummy" and write, "Thanks so much, and I hope to hear from you soon."*

> NOTE: Only be conversational if you developed a comfortable back-and-forth with the interviewer. Otherwise, play it safe.

– Your first name

Email signature

_____

Deeper Insight

It's important to gauge the situation, but always try to be personable and remind the manager or interviewer you paid attention. Minor details make your email stand out even more.

If you have the time, send a handwritten note and still include the same level of detail. The move will bring you closer to the gold medal: a job offer.

QUICK TIP — The secret to a strong job search subject line

You know what happens to emails with vague subject lines?

Nothing. That's what.

People may not open the email at all. And when you circle back to check if the person saw your message, the answer is something like, "Oh, maybe it went to spam. Please send again."

The email didn't go to spam. The subject line was so unexceptional the person never noticed it.

The secret to a GREAT subject line? Specifics.

Instead of "Job application" you write, "James Seevers, application for product analyst position."

Instead of "Follow up" you write, "James Seevers, follow up on product analyst position."

Instead of "Thank you" you write, "Thanks for today's interview at Starbucks."

Every time you write a subject line, include the information below if it's relevant to the situation:

- ▶ Your first and last name
- ▶ Job title you want
- ▶ Where/when you had an interview or conversation
- ▶ Month/day ("January 24") if time has passed since the meeting/conversation, and you need to remind the person about when you spoke

All the specifics make your subject quicker to spot and easier to understand. Don't make people scan their brains to remember you; put all the relevant info in one line.

Response Emails

HOW TO REPLY WHEN YOU DON'T LAND THE JOB/INTERNSHIP

The scenario: The employer sends the "Sorry you didn't land the job" email and, too disappointed or angry at the outcome, you don't reply. You go dark and think, "Who needs that company, anyway? Moving on."

Bad idea. Why?

No reply: you leave zero opportunity on the table.

A prompt answer: anything can happen.

What if:

▸ the person the company chooses ultimately doesn't take the job?

▸ the company decides to hire two people and not one?

▸ some unforeseen circumstance requires the company to reopen the job search?

If you and another person were finalists for the job, your follow-up email might have an impact. You stood tall and took the rejection. The other person, feeling spurned, walked away.

The next time you get a big fat "No," send off this reply:

Hi _____,

Thank you for letting me know about the [name of position/internship]. I understand your decision and appreciate the opportunity to interview for the job.

Please keep me in mind for future opportunities, even in a freelance capacity. I respect the work you do at [name of company] and would like to contribute if possible.

NOTE: Advanced skill: Add this line before "All the best":

"I maintain a personal hashtag, #yournameportfolio, where I post articles I find interesting and the latest on my career. Please check it out from time to time and see what I'm doing."

If you have a blog/website, you can include a link there as well.

All the best,

– Your first name

Email signature

Deeper Insight

Roll with the rejection and see if you can maintain the relationship with the company — if it's still a place where you would like to work.

How to tell people who helped you network that you landed the job

Often, we land a job through the help of people in our network. A friend mentions you to a hiring manager. A former boss puts in a good word with the potential new boss. A friend "on the inside" passes along your resume.

If you do secure the job, make sure all the people who pitched in learn the good news.

Subject line: Update on [job title] position at [name of company]

Hi [name of person who helped you],

Good morning/afternoon.

I found out [today/this week] I landed the [name of position] job at [name of company]. I'm excited to get started!

NOTE: Great news deserves an exclamation!

[If you have information on the job, start date and/or your expected role, let the person know; for instance, "I will start on December 3, and in the job I will primarily assist the executive team with upcoming client seminars in Denver and Colorado Springs."]

Thank you again for [how did the person help? For instance, "bringing my resume to the attention of CFO Dean Verdinas. Your recommendation made a huge difference"].

> NOTE: Remind your friend of the exact way he/she helped you and use full names ("CFO Dean Verdinas") when available.

If there's anything I can do for you, please let me know. I'm happy to lend a hand.

Thanks,

– Your first name

Email signature

Deeper Insight

The person who helped you will be thrilled to know you found a job. Plus, the person might have additional perspective on the company where you will work or the kind of tasks you will do. Keep the conversation going and continue to build on the relationship.

How to tell people who helped you network that you didn't land the job

Even if you strike out with the job you want, it's important to update the people who helped you network. Otherwise, how will they know to keep looking for opportunities for you?

Subject line: Update on [job title] position at [name of company]

Hi [name of person who helped you],

Good morning/afternoon.

I found out [today/this week] I did not land the job as a/an [job title] at [name of company].

[If you know why you didn't get the job and want to explain, do so here; for instance, "I made it to the final round of interviews but was told I don't have enough research experience. I think the person they did hire has already been published in two scholarly journals."]

Thank you again for [how did the person help? For instance, "reaching out and connecting me with Joan Woltham, the hiring manager"].

> NOTE: Remind your friend of the exact way he/she helped you and use full names ("Joan Woltham") when available.

I will continue my search and keep you posted on my progress. If there's anything I can do for you in the meantime, please let me know. I'm happy to lend a hand.

Thanks,

– Your first name

Email signature

Deeper Insight

Be thankful for the assistance and honest about why you didn't land the job. Also offer to help the other person. Giving makes the world go 'round.

How to turn down an internship

If you can't accept the internship, be up front about your decision but also leave the door open for future ways to engage with the company or organization.

Subject line: Internship opportunity at [name of company/organization]

Hi _____,

Good morning/good afternoon.

Thanks again for taking the time to meet with me.

I have decided not to accept the internship at [company/organization]. I appreciate the opportunity, but [explain why you can't do the internship; for instance, "my course load is too busy this semester, and I don't have the time to also work as an intern"].

> NOTE: If you want to stay in contact, add a line like: "I will be in touch when my schedule allows for an internship because I would love to spend time with your team and learn the business."

All the best with the search,

– Your first name

Email signature

Deeper Insight

Even though you can't fulfill the internship right now, that's no reason to say "See you later" forever. Look to maintain a relationship with a person at the company so he/she might consider you (or give you favorable treatment) when you do want to intern or perhaps apply for a job.

How to turn down a job offer

The company wants you, but you need to say "No" in the nicest way possible. Here's how.

Subject line: Position of [job title]

Hi _____,

Good [morning/afternoon].

Thank you for offering me the position of [job title]. After careful consideration, I have concluded it is not the right opportunity at this time and decided to decline your offer.

Thanks for the time and consideration you've given me throughout the process. I enjoyed getting to know you and others on the team.

> NOTE: You may have other information to include like details on where you accepted a job or another person the company should consider for the position. If so, add the information here.

All the best with the search,

– Your first name

Email signature

Deeper Insight

Let the person know you appreciate how much time he/she may have spent with you during the rounds of interviews.

Even if you need to turn down the job, it's important to maintain a healthy relationship with the employer. You never know when you might run into him/her again down the road.

How to make sure the company received your job application

You send off a job application, don't receive a reply and wonder if anyone at the company saw it.

After two to three business days without an answer, consider the email below.

Subject line: [Your first and last name], follow up on job application for [job title] position

Hi _____,

> NOTE: I know there's a lot of frustration today over a perceived "black hole" for online job postings, in which the company never responds and says, "Thanks, we have your application."
>
> Rather than wait around for an answer, consider (if you can find it) an email to a person involved in the hiring process, an email to a general address like info@company.com or a message through a contact form.

This week, I applied for the position of _____. I sent it to you on [month/day].

If possible, please let me know if you have my application. I am happy to answer any additional questions.

Thanks again for the opportunity,

– Your first name

Email signature

Deeper Insight

What if you receive no response to the follow-up email after 48 hours? Your next line of attack is to call the company's main number and say:

You: Hi, my name is _____, and [earlier this week/last week] I applied for the position of _____. I am calling to make sure you received my application.

Are you the right person to talk to or should I speak with someone else?

The best case scenario is to find someone in the company who promises to look into your application. In a small way, it means you then have an advocate "on the inside," which is better than applying as a complete stranger.

If the employer confirms he/she received your application, you have two more reasons to feel good:

▸ you don't have to worry your application is lost in the shuffle

▸ you've shown the employer you know how to follow through

How to reply when the employer writes, "We have your application, thanks"

Two scenarios for the follow-up email below:

1. If you apply for a job online and a person writes, "We have your application, thanks."
2. If you check on the status of the application and a person writes, "We have your application and will let you know if we need more information or want to schedule an interview."

In either case, you can reply with:

"Thanks so much for letting me know you received my application, [person's first name]. I appreciate the response."

– Your first name

Email signature

NOTE: Make sure you have a link in the email signature to your blog, online portfolio or #personalhashtag. Then you potentially give the person a way to learn more about you as he/she reviews applications.

Deeper Insight

In most cases, I would try to take the conversation further than a traditional response. For instance, I would link to a highlight from my portfolio.

Here, it's too risky. Keep your answer straightforward and don't use the email to talk about your career or engage in a back-and-forth conversation. Unless the person asks for examples of your work, play it cool and save the deeper discussion in case you land an interview.

That's why you put a link to your blog or portfolio in the email signature and on your cover letter/resume. Even if the person doesn't ask to see your work, he/she might still be curious enough to click on your link in the signature. It's a subtle way to say, "Look if you want."

How to reply when the employer writes, "Your interview is scheduled for..."

Ever seen an email like this one? I bet you have.

> "Hi [your name],
>
> Your interview is scheduled for Thursday, April 9 at 2:30 p.m. with John Geere, our director of operations. We'll see you then."
>
> Angela Rockwell
> Executive Assistant
> Acme Corporation

How do you reply? Typically two ways:

- Respond with a simple "OK thanks"
- Don't answer at all (bad idea)

Instead, send an email in which you re-confirm the day and time of your meeting.

"Thanks so much, Angela. I look forward to meeting Mr. Geere on Thursday, April 9 at 2:30 p.m. I'll see him then."

NOTE: More on why you should be a name dropper on page 24.

Deeper Insight

A secretary or other staffer who schedules interviews might also make recommendations when it's time to hire someone. You need to impress every person you contact at the company.

QUICK TIP — Use the right words to defeat resume-scanning robots

Look at a job description. What keywords do you think a hiring manager looks for with an Applicant Tracking System (ATS)?

It's not predictable adjectives like "successful" and "hardworking." Although I can't say for sure an employer NEVER looks for those words, it's unlikely.

Why? If an employer ONLY searches for the typical words EVERYONE uses, then the ATS would show EVERYONE in the results.

Employers seek people with "hard" skills. Software programs, tools, hands-on know-how (ex: CPR certified). They often want to narrow down the applicant pool based on what people can physically do on the job.

As you compose a resume or cover letter, look at the job description and ask yourself:

▸ What skills and abilities does the company value?

> *NOTE: I don't mean only technical skills like software and certifications. If the position requires someone who can "work independently," then include those two words in your application. That's more specific than if you write "hardworking," and it could be a phrase used in the ATS.*

▸ Does it seem like the company focuses primarily on one or two skills?
▸ How can I weave those terms and keywords into my own application?

An ATS falls right in line with the lessons I hope to impart in the book. Tangible skills set us apart.

A job description is a blueprint and explains what the company wants in a new hire. If you have the skills a company values (ex: tools, software and certifications), then make sure those words are in your application.

Robot or no robot, the most qualified (AKA "most skilled") candidates stand the best chance.

Making Connections

HOW TO ASK FOR A LETTER OF RECOMMENDATION

The line below — or something similar — probably graces every one of your recommendation letters:

"I had the privilege of working with [your name] and believe he/she is one of the most promising young people I have ever met."

Sorry to break it to you, but other applicants have nearly identical recommendation letters. That's because everyone writes cookie-cutter endorsements full of flowery compliments.

The employer, in turn, reads letter after letter that looks and sounds the same. The silly little game needs to stop and here's how it can:

Ask the recommendation person to tell a story about you

People don't care about your work ethic unless they understand HOW you work hard. A short story about success on the job will impress an employer more than anything else.

Subject line: Request for a letter of recommendation

Hi _____,

I hope you're doing well.

132

[Ask a question specific to the person's career; for instance, "How is everything going at Acme Corporation? Do you have a solid group of interns this time around?"]

I am applying for [tell the person what you're up to; for instance, "a master's in fashion studies at Big State University in New York City" or "a sales position at Big Corporation in New York City"].

NOTE: Tell the recommendation person where you want to go to school or work. Why? Maybe he/she attended Big State University or worked at Big Corporation. Then the person might be able to put in a word for you. Always stress the details.

Would you be able to write a letter of recommendation for me? If so, I think the [boss, hiring manager, etc...] would like to know about the time I [your story; for instance, "ran all over NYC to gather different types of flowers for the outdoor garden photo shoot. That day is a great example of my hustle and focus."]

NOTE: Give the person a story to tell about you. Also, provide details to jog the person's memory and explain why you want the reference letter to include the story (it will "help me stand out").

The recommendation doesn't need to be long. A couple of paragraphs will be fine, and I hope a specific story will help me stand out.

Thanks so much,

– Your first name

Email signature

Deeper Insight

If you can't think of a specific story or don't feel comfortable asking for one, write: "If a particular situation comes to mind, feel free to share it. I know employers would like to see an example of my abilities."

Allow the person 48 hours to respond. If no answer, follow up with, "I want to make sure you saw my email the other day about a recommendation letter. Please let me know and thanks again."

For a template on how to say "Thanks" for the letter of recommendation, see the guide on page 185.

How to follow up with an employer you met at a job fair

You had a conversation with an employer at a job fair. Terrific. Now what?

The same day or the following morning, keep the dialogue going.

Subject line: Follow up, [your first and last name] from the [name of job fair]

Hi _____,

It was great to meet you earlier today at the [name of job fair].

After we spoke, I did more research on [name of company]. I find the work you do interesting, particularly [one or two projects listed on the website; for instance, "your data analytics project for the military. That must be inspiring work at such a critical time for our country"].

NOTE: Don't launch into a request for a follow-up conversation. Show you care about the company first.

I have attached my resume to this email so you have an online copy.

Please let me know if we can talk again. I want to learn more about the company and how I can be an asset to your team. As I mentioned yesterday, [remind the person about your expertise or specialty if you have one; for instance, "I have three years of experience building landing pages and tracking sales data for a national retailer"].

Thanks again, and I hope to hear from you.

– Your first name

Email signature

Deeper Insight

A recruiter could meet hundreds of people at a job fair. How many will send an email once the fair is over? A small number.

Moreover, you studied up on the company after the initial conversation and referenced a recent project. At the end, you also remind the person why your skill set matches what the company may need.

With every layer of detail, the email becomes more valuable.

How to network with someone you met at a job fair

Let's say you strike up a conversation with someone interesting at the job fair. Even if the person can't offer you a job, send an email within 24 hours to explore how you might work together or network further.

Subject line: Follow up, [first and last name] from the [name of job fair]

Hi _____,

It was great to meet you earlier today at the [name of job fair].

After we spoke, I did more research on [name of company]. I find the work you do interesting, particularly the [one or two projects listed on the website; for instance, "your <u>new technology to track cargo freight</u> more efficiently. That seems like a powerful tool and will give your team an edge"].

Then, a few options:

1. If the person can help you find a job:

As I said yesterday, I am in the job market and appreciate any help you can provide. My quick bio: [one or two lines on your career so the person can potentially pass your info to someone else; for instance, "I recently finished my time in the Navy and am looking for a job in IT. I oversaw IT and data management the past four years aboard an aircraft carrier, the USS Acme, and hope to do similar work in the private sector. I have attached my resume to this email so you have an online copy"].

> *NOTE: Don't be vague and write, "I recently finished my time in the Navy." Use specifics like "oversaw IT and data management" and "USS Acme." The details make you more interesting.*

2. If the person can connect you with someone else:

You mentioned there might be an opportunity at [name of company]. Are you able to send a short email and introduce me? I am also happy to send the message on my own if you give me an email address. I attached my resume to this email so you have an online copy.

> *NOTE: Offer to write the intro email yourself to take the burden off the other person.*

3. If you want to stay in touch as a networking strategy:

It would be great to meet up again and [why you want to get together; for instance, "explore how our two businesses can work together. How about coffee sometime over the next week? Please let me know"].

I have attached my resume to this email so you have an online copy.

Thanks again,

– Your first name

Email signature

Deeper Insight

No matter the reason for the email, you should stay in touch with notable people you meet at job fairs. Keep your circle wide to maximize career opportunities.

How to ask someone you know for help with the job search

If you're at a crossroads and need career guidance, rely on people you know and trust with the email below.

Subject line: In the job market, need your advice

NOTE: In my experience, 99 percent of people like when someone asks for their advice. What an ego boost!

Hi _____,

Hope you're doing well. [Ask a question about the other person; for instance, "How is everything at Acme Corporation? What's up with the robot pet project?"]

I'm in the job market and could use your help as I [brainstorm opportunities/ network with people in the industry/plan my next career move].

To remind you, I [catch the person up; for instance, "left my job at Intel in March and hope to find something new in the local tech scene"]. I have attached my resume to this email.

NOTE: You don't need a lengthy explanation on why you're looking for a new job. Save the monologue for the actual conversation and keep the message brief.

Are you free this week or next to talk with me? It would be great to meet in person if you're available.

NOTE: In-person meetings trump phone calls. Push for a face-to-face conversation.

Please let me know and thanks so much,

– Your first name

Email signature

Deeper Insight

Ask how the other person is doing, explain what you hope to accomplish in your conversation and give the person two full weeks of potential days to meet or speak by phone.

At the meeting itself, bring your resume, a way to take notes and a list of questions so you can probe the person's career. For help with the questions, go to page 221.

How to ask someone you don't know for help with the job search

If you want career guidance from someone you don't know, your email must have an explanation of who you are and how you found the person.

Subject line: In the job market, need your advice

> *NOTE: The "ask for advice" route is crucial if the person doesn't know you. Otherwise, the person might not open your email at all since he/she doesn't recognize the name of the sender.*

Hi _____,

My name is [first and last name], and I am a [put yourself in context; for instance, "recent political science graduate from Big State"]. I hope you're doing well.

I [found/received] your email address from [how you know this person; for instance, "Jim Stevens, a fellow Big State University alumnus who worked with you at Acme Corporation. Jim thought I should make introductions and network a bit." OR you could say something like "the Big State University alumni database and thought I would reach out"].

> *NOTE: Be 100 percent clear about how you found this person.*

I'm in the job market and could use your help as I [brainstorm opportunities/ network with people in the industry/plan my next career move; for instance, "consider a career switch and go into accounting. I'd like to learn more about the job and how I should enter the field"].

Are you free this week or next to talk with me? It would be great to meet in person if you're available.

> *NOTE: In-person meetings trump phone calls. Push for a face-to-face conversation.*

Please let me know and thanks so much,

– Your first name

Email signature

Deeper Insight

Like the template on page 137, check in on the other person, make clear what you want from the conversation and see if the person is free over the next two weeks.

At the meeting, remember to bring copies of your resume, a way to take notes and several questions to examine the person's career. For questions to ask, check out page 221.

How to ask someone you worked under to be a reference

You'll need a bit of small talk for the email below. Don't begin your request without a little chit-chat first.

Subject line: Need your help as a reference

Hi _____,

[Check in on the other person with a question about his/her life; for instance, "How is everything going at Acme Corporation? Gearing up for another busy season?"]

I am in the job market and want to have references ready in case I need them. Could I list you as a reference? It would be a big help.

If so, give me your best phone number and email address. Also, do I have your job title correct?

[List the person's job title and company]

> NOTE: Never assume you know the person's job title and company. Always double check contact details.

Please let me know and thanks so much,

– Your first name

Email signature

Deeper Insight

Unless directed, leave references off your resume. They aren't necessary and take up space. The employer will ask for them at the appropriate time.

How to ask someone you didn't work under to be a reference

Sometimes we need a reference from someone we didn't work for or under. No big deal. The template is much the same as the one on the previous page except it explains your connection.

Subject line: Need your help as a reference

Hi _____,

[Check in on the other person with a question about his/her life; for instance, "How is everything going in the 3D printing business? Is the product becoming more popular with business owners?"]

I am in the job market and want to have references ready in case I need them. I know we never worked together, but I think you could speak to my work ethic because [explain why; for instance, "of the time we collaborated at the Salem conference and organized all the speakers and workshops"].

NOTE: Since technically you never worked together, you need to explain why you want the person to serve as a reference.

Could I list you as a reference? It would be a big help.

If so, give me your best phone number and email address.

Also, do I have your job title correct?

[List the person's job title and company]

Please let me know what you can do and thanks so much.

– Your first name

Email signature

Deeper Insight

Again, leave references off your resume unless otherwise directed.

QUICK TIP — How to title documents like resumes and cover letters

When you send documents like a cover letter and resume, how should you title the files? Yes, I mean the actual file names on your computer.

It looks sloppy when you attach a file like:

- myresume.docx
- mycoverletter1.docx

Plus, a generic title for a resume could be problematic. What if the hiring manager receives 75 resumes called "myresume.docx"?

You don't want to be tossed in with everyone else, right? I didn't think so.

Here's the formula for professional documents:

[Name of document] for [your first and last name] — position of [job title]

So it would be:

- Resume for Mark Simpson — position of account executive
- Cover letter for Mark Simpson — position of account executive
- Portfolio for Mark Simpson — position of account executive

NOTE: Remember we don't capitalize job titles ("account executive") unless they come right before our name.

Formal name vs nickname

What if your formal name is Robert but your coworkers call you "Robby"? Should you go by "Robby Ramirez" on your job applications?

I say no. Stick with your formal name in professional situations like a resume, cover letter and on LinkedIn. And yes, my own resume has "Daniel Rubin" at the top.

Why? "Robby" might be a mature, responsible guy any company would be lucky to have. Until the hiring manager or supervisor becomes familiar with Robby, the nickname makes him seem young and inexperienced. Plus, you never know who might review your application, and you need to be polished.

▸ Resume for **Robby** Ramirez

Vs

▸ Resume for **Robert** Ramirez

Which person looks more mature on paper?
Exactly.

Informational interviews

HOW TO ASK AS A RECENT GRAD WITH NO CONNECTION AT THE COMPANY

You're fresh out of school and need to explore a job, industry or other opportunity. To make the situation tougher, you don't know anyone at the company.

Subject line: Recent graduate from [name of school], request for informational interview

Hi _____,

My name is [first and last name], and I'm a [put yourself in context; for instance, "recent sociology graduate from _____"]. It's nice to meet you.

If possible, I would like to schedule a quick informational interview so I can learn more about [name of company].

> NOTE: Make your "ask" early in the email so the person knows what you want.

At [college/university], I majored in [field the employer would find relevant] and hope to work in the same field. In school, I often worked on/with [one or two topics or "hard" skills you learned; for instance, "Software Tool 1 and Software Tool 2"] and am ready to put those skills to use.

[If you have a link to a blog or online portfolio, add a line like, "Here's a link to my portfolio, which has several examples of my work."]

I read about your background and see you [one or two highlights from the person's career — look at a website bio or LinkedIn profile; for instance, "began as an intern at Big Corporation and rose to become a senior vice president. It's inspiring for someone like me who has started out in the field"].

> NOTE: Use specific words like the person's company, job title or project. Prove you did your research.

Again, please let me know if you have a few minutes to meet. I would appreciate the chance to ask questions about the [name of industry; for instance, "education"] field and learn more about your own path.

I have also attached my resume.

Thanks so much,

– Your first name

Email signature

Deeper Insight

Who could ignore such a genuine, thoughtful email?

Focus on the person's career so he/she can pass along wisdom and make you better. Hopefully, the person will take you up on the offer. If not, try someone else with the same approach.

How to ask as a recent grad with a connection at the company

Isn't life easier when you have connections? The email below, unlike the one where you don't know anyone at the company, allows you to make a more seamless introduction.

Subject line: Friend of [person who connects you two], request for informational interview

Hi _____,

My name is [first and last name], and I'm [reference the way you two are connected; for instance, "Don Cunningham's son"]. It's nice to meet you.

[Your connection] thought I should make introductions and let you know I recently graduated from [name of college/university]. I have a degree in _____ and am interested in a job in the [field you want to work in] field. If possible, I'd like to come by your office for a quick informational interview to learn more about the company and the industry, in general.

> NOTE: Ask for the meeting early in the email so a busy person knows what you want right away.

At [college/university], I often worked on/with [one or two topics or "hard" skills you learned; for instance, "Software Tool 1 and Software Tool 2"] and am ready to put those skills to use.

NOTE: Don't drop bland buzzwords like "hardworking" and "dedicated." Reference actual skills, tools and software. That's what counts.

[If you have a link to a blog or online portfolio, add a line like, "Here's a link to my portfolio, which has several examples of my work.]

I read about your background and see [one or two highlights from the person's career — look at the website bio or LinkedIn profile; for instance, "how you lead the company's design team and last year won national honors for your ad campaign about childhood obesity. It's a powerful ad that made me stop and think"].

Again, please let me know if you have a few minutes to meet. I would appreciate the chance to ask questions about the [name of industry; for instance, "health care"] field and learn more about your career path.

Thanks so much,

– Your first name

Email signature

Deeper Insight

Don't take a connection for granted. You must still show you researched the person's career and company and provide examples of your work, if available.

How to ask if you're unemployed with no connection at the company

If you've been out of the work world a bit (not a recent graduate) and need an informational interview, here's how to start the conversation.

Subject line: [Job title; for instance, "Marketing professional"], request for informational interview

Hi _____,

My name is [first and last name], and I'm a [put yourself in context; for instance, "marketing professional here in Boise"]. It's nice to meet you.

I'm writing to see if we can meet for a brief informational interview so I can learn more about [name of company].

> NOTE: Be clear about what you want right from the get-go. Don't make a busy person scan the email to learn your intentions.

At my most recent company, [name of company], I handled [your primary role; for instance, "the company's digital portfolio, which included campaigns for local banks, law firms and restaurants. Here's a link to my online portfolio"].

[Then, why you want to check out the company; for instance, "I like what your team is doing with data analytics and think I can add value in the space. At Acme Corporation, I developed a way to manage data and began to weave the findings into our client projects."]

[If you feel it's necessary or appropriate to explain why you're out of work, do so here; for instance, "To give you the background, Acme Corporation had a round of job cuts in late October so now I'm in search of new opportunities."]

> NOTE: Don't include an explanation about why you're out of a job if it will hurt your chances ("I was fired because...")

I read about your career and see you [one or two highlights from the person's career — look at the website bio or LinkedIn profile; for instance,

147

"worked on Madison Avenue in NYC for a large ad agency. That must have been a cool experience, and I'd like to hear more about it"].

Again, please let me know if you have a few minutes to meet. I would appreciate the chance to ask questions about the company and learn more about your career path.

Thanks so much,

– Your first and last name

Email signature

Deeper Insight

You must craft an email that proves you care about the company and not as though you sent the same message to 50 different businesses. Make it authentic.

How to ask if you're unemployed with a connection at the company

If you have an "in" with someone at the company, leverage the relationship to hopefully schedule an informational interview.

Subject line: Friend of [person who connects you two], request for informational interview

Hi _____,

My name is [first and last name], and I'm [reference the way you two are connected; for instance, "Jovan Wright's friend"]. It's nice to meet you.

[Name of your connection] thought I should make introductions and let you know I'm a [job title] and looking for a job in the [name of industry; for instance, "automotive"] field. If possible, I'd like to come by your office for a brief informational interview to learn more about the company and the work you do.

> NOTE: "Brief" is the optimal word. Let the person know right away you don't plan to take up the entire day.

At my most recent job as a [job title] for [name of company], I handled [your primary role; for instance, "inventory management for three car part distribution sites in the Akron area"].

[If you have a link to a blog or online portfolio, add a line like, "Here's a link to my portfolio with several examples of my work."]

[If you feel it's necessary or appropriate to explain why you're out of work, do so here; for instance, "To give you the background, Acme Corporation made budget cuts this past June and laid people off so now I'm in search of new opportunities."]

> NOTE: Don't include an explanation about why you're out of a job if it will hurt your chances ("I was fired because…")

I read about your career and see you [one or two highlights from the person's career — look at the website bio or LinkedIn profile; for instance, "have worked hard to integrate robotic technology with traditional inventory management processes. I am interested in a work environment like that — a place on the cutting edge"].

Again, please let me know if you have a few minutes to meet. I would appreciate the chance to ask questions about [name of company] and learn more about your career path.

Thanks so much,

– Your first name

Email signature

Deeper Insight

Unlike the email with no connection, this time you and the person who receives the email know someone in common. Right away, you have the person's trust and (you'd hope) willingness to meet.

Still, show the person you researched his/her career and don't take the time for granted.

How to thank someone after an informational interview

Within 24 hours of the informational interview (and ideally the same day), send a note to thank the person for the time and insight.

DO NOT overlook the thank-you note. You could waste all the goodwill you built up in the meeting if you don't send a note after it's over.

Subject line: Thanks again for your time

Hi _____,

Thanks again for meeting with me this [morning/afternoon]. I appreciate your time and enjoyed learning more about the company.

[Then a line from your conversation; for instance, "Seems like your team is doing such exciting work right now. After we talked about your expansion into the Phoenix suburbs, I went on your website and read more. I think you're right that suburban Phoenix is ready for your clothing line."]

> NOTE: A little small talk in the email can go a long way. Be conversational and don't jump to what you want: the person to connect you with a job or other people he/she knows who might need to make a hire.

I have attached my resume to the email. Please let me know if there's someone you can connect me to about a job opportunity. I am happy to make the introduction myself if you pass along an email address.

[Or if the person mentioned someone he/she could connect you to, write: "Please let me know if you're able to connect me with _____. An introduction from you would be helpful."]

Thanks and have a great day,

– Your first name

Email signature

Deeper Insight

The thank-you note should reference your conversation. It's all about managing expectations. The person expects you to send a basic note with, "Thanks a lot. Please let me know if any opportunities arise at your company."

Even though it's an "informational" interview, the person can now think of you for open positions at the company or at places where he/she has colleagues. Make a strong first impression, and it might lead to something great down the road.

Engage with Recruiters

HOW TO TELL A RECRUITER YOU'RE INTERESTED IN A JOB

If you want to capture the attention of a recruiter for a particular job, send a strong introductory email and make a great first impression.

Subject line: Interested in position of [job title} at [name of company]

Hi Mr./Ms. _____[be formal with a recruiter],

I am reaching out because I saw the posting for [job title] at [name of company]. After I researched the position and company, I feel I would be a great fit for the opportunity.

I believe I have the required skills and would mesh well with the culture at [name of company]. In particular, I like how the company [something

151

notable from the website, news or a line from the mission statement; for instance, "believes in leveraging new technology to help people live healthier lives"].

[Then, give an example of why you have the proper skills and, if possible, why you're a good cultural fit; for instance, "I am proficient with JavaScript and HTML5, and I also have experience working with virtual teams, as I know that's an important part of how the company operates."]

> NOTE: If the job description lists required skills and experience you don't have, you will gain credibility by addressing them; for instance, "I noted the job description also requires experience implementing Acme's Business Intelligence tool. While I do not have that direct experience, I was selected to lead the implementation of an enterprise-wide database and was able to keep the project on time and under budget."

I have attached my resume to this email. I'd also be happy to provide a cover letter if additional information would be helpful. Finally, I'm open to your feedback on my candidacy and overall portfolio.

> NOTE: Ask for feedback because it allows the recruiter to engage in a dialogue with you, which may help to build trust and deepen your relationship.

Thanks, and I hope to hear from you.

– Your first and last name

Email signature

Deeper Insight

With the introductory email to a recruiter, you need to explain why you're not only technically skilled but also someone who would be a solid teammate. A recruiter needs a person who can operate on both levels. Also, ask for feedback and be appreciative whether it's positive or negative.

If the position requires relocation, indicate what draws you to the city. Recruiters often pay more attention to candidates from out of state who have a connection to the job location (ex: family ties).

How to thank a recruiter after an interview or initial screen

Once the conversation is over, send off a polished thank-you message the recruiter won't soon forget.

Subject line: Thanks for your time [this morning/this afternoon]

Hi Mr./Ms. _____ [be formal with a recruiter unless, during the interview, the person says, "You can call me by my first name"],

Thanks again for talking with me [this morning/this afternoon] about the [job title] position at [name of company].

> NOTE: A recruiter might talk to several candidates in a single day for multiple positions and companies. Always reiterate the job and company that relate to you.

I appreciate the questions you asked and the opportunity to discuss my career.

[Here's a free space to include something memorable. It could be:

- an additional piece of info about your career: "To clarify, I have project management experience as well as billing/admin experience."

- a link to a page you want the person to see: "Here's my portfolio with more examples of my design work."

- a critique from the recruiter you respect: "Thanks for helping me understand what employers in the aerospace industry need today. That's terrific insight."]

Please let me know if I can provide any additional information.

Thanks and have a great day,

– Your first and last name

Email signature

Deeper Insight

The keys with the thank-you email are to remind the recruiter what job you're after and reference a moment or detail from the conversation. It will help to encourage the recruiter to respond and remember you for the position you want or another one down the road.

How to follow up on a hiring decision

After the interview rounds and as you wait on "the answer," here's a polite way to check back in.

Subject line: Checking in, decision on [job title] at [name of company]

Hi Mr./Ms. _____ [be formal with a recruiter unless, during the interview, the person says, "You can call me by my first name"],

Good morning/afternoon.

I'm checking on the status of the [job title] position at [name of company]. If you have a chance, please let me know where my candidacy stands.

Thanks again for your help,

– Your first and last name

Email signature

Deeper Insight

Short and to the point. Nicely drop in, see if you can glean any new information and then hit "Send." Wait 1–2 days and if you receive no response, consider one more follow-up message like, "Hi _____, I want to follow up one more time on the [job title] position at [name of company]. Any information you can provide would be helpful. Thanks again."

How to respond to a rejection

The recruiter emails and explains you didn't land the job. Bummer, I know. But keep your head high and come right back with a message that shows you're grateful for the opportunity and ready for whatever comes next.

Hi Mr./Ms. _____ [be formal with a recruiter unless, during the interview, the person says, "You can call me by my first name"],

Thanks for the email and for letting me know about the job. I appreciate it.

While I'm disappointed I wasn't selected, I hope you'll keep me in mind for future opportunities. [Then, a line specific to the type of job or field where you hope to work; for instance, "I am open to more jobs in the IT field that draw on my knowledge of UX."]

I also welcome any feedback or critiques on my job application and how I came across in the interview process.

I'd welcome staying in touch from time to time to hear about other opportunities, and I'd be happy to provide referrals or any assistance with other searches you conduct.

> NOTE: Be open to criticism. What if you didn't dress well for the interview, and it doomed your chances? You need to know so you can correct the mistake. Plus, if you ask the recruiter for advice, it could help foster a relationship in a mentor/mentee kind of way.

Thanks again, and have a great day/night.

– Your first and last name

Email signature

Deeper Insight

Be gracious and ask for constructive criticism. How else will you improve? Maybe you were a finalist for the position and the recruiter likes you a lot. That means you could be in a good place for the next relevant job the recruiter needs to fill. Relationships are everything.

Chapter 5
LinkedIn Templates

Grow Your Network

LinkedIn is a giant professional playground with millions of people ready and willing to network. Otherwise, why would they have created profiles?

As you start conversations on LinkedIn, apply the same principles from the sections on networking and the job search.

1. Networking: be curious about other people.
2. Job search: provide detailed information about your career.

With LinkedIn, you also need to take diligent care of your own profile, which leads me to two points.

3. LinkedIn profile summary: tell people why you're passionate about the work you do or hope to do.

4. LinkedIn profile work experience: use specifics to demonstrate success.

Now let's hop into the sandbox and get our hands dirty.

HOW TO SEND EFFECTIVE LINKEDIN INVITES

We send and receive LinkedIn "invites" so often, we forget we can customize the message inside the invitation.

LinkedIn automatically gives us:

I'd like to add you to my professional network on LinkedIn.

– Your first and last name

The next time you send an invite from a computer, request to connect from within the person's profile page. Then you can write a custom message.

▸ If you met the person somewhere and want to connect on LinkedIn, go with:

"Great to meet you at [place where you met]. Let's stay in touch!"

▸ If you saw/read/heard the person and liked what he/she is all about, go with:

"I enjoyed [how you came across the person; for instance, 'your interview about children and nutrition on the radio']. Let's stay in touch!"

▸ If you find the person's LinkedIn profile interesting, go with:

"I enjoyed reading about your [what you find notable on the person's profile, 'experience with 3D printing here in Milwaukee']. Let's stay in touch!"

Finally, if you want to invite the person to set up a conversation, you can remove "Let's stay in touch!" and add "I'd like to set up a time to talk over the next couple of weeks. Please let me know if you're free. Thanks!" You will need to judge the scenario and if it's appropriate to ask for the person's time.

Here's what happens when you turn the LinkedIn invite into a special note:

The person may respond with a special note too.

If you use the template LinkedIn provides, there's little chance for a reply. Your message looks no different from all the others. Why bother with an answer?

A personal invite could start a conversation and lead to a business relationship. All it takes is a willingness to go "one layer deeper," as we discuss on page 20.

How to write a networking message

LinkedIn has now made private messages more like a back-and-forth conversation. If you press "Enter" to start a new line, your text is automatically sent. That's why you should draft these messages somewhere else (ex: Microsoft Word) and then transfer everything at once.

Subject line: Hope to connect with you

Hi _____,

My name is [first and last name], and I'm [put yourself in context; for instance, "a friend of Melissa Hardy, who thought I should introduce myself"].

I am reaching out because [state what you want in one or two sentences; for instance, "In April my company, Acme Corporation, finished 'Big Green,' a documentary on the marijuana industry, and the film might be a great fit for your independent movie theater in Ft. Lauderdale"].

NOTE: Put your "purpose" at the top of the message so the person sees it right away.

[If you have more information about the request, include it here and consider bullet points to make everything easy to read.]

[Then, reference a couple of facts from the person's LinkedIn profile to prove you studied up before you sent the message; for instance, "I read your LinkedIn profile and see you're a big fan of independent films produced here in the US. I also noticed you list 'home brewing' as an interest so hopefully you'd like a film about counter cultures."]

NOTE: The person puts his/her entire bio right at your fingertips. There's no excuse if you leave out a section on why you find the person's career compelling.

Please let me know if there's a time over the next two weeks for us to talk.

Thanks, and I hope to hear from you.

– Your first and last name

Deeper Insight

State your purpose at the top of the message and reference details from the person's LinkedIn profile. Make the email authentic (even though the person might be a stranger) to build trust and give yourself a better chance at a reply.

How to network with someone who sent you a connection

If someone you don't know asks to connect on LinkedIn — and you think the person is worth a further conversation — send back a message, be curious and explore. What's the point of LinkedIn if not to meet people who cross our paths?

Subject line: Thanks for the connection

Hi _____,

I'm [first and last name], a [job title] at [company if you're employed] in [city]. Nice to meet you.

NOTE: Provide a full introduction rather than only your name.

Thanks for connecting with me. I enjoyed reading more about your career, especially [one item you find interesting and a question about it; for instance, "how you rose through the ranks at Acme Corporation to become a chief designer. What's the project you consider your favorite?"].

I'm not sure if you looked over my profile, but you might be interested in my [what you want the person to know; for instance, "animation experience on special projects. Here's a quick example of my work: add URL here"].

[Then, what do you want from the other person? For instance: "Could I ask you a few questions about the hiring process at Acme Corporation and how I can compose a winning job application? Please let me know if you have time for a quick call."]

> NOTE: You could have all kinds of questions for the person, but keep your request focused and to the point.

Thanks,

– Your first and last name

Deeper Insight

If someone connects on LinkedIn with YOU, then why not send a quick message, network and see if there are ways to work together or collaborate?

If you receive no response but feel it's a relationship you need to pursue, wait 48 hours and reply back with, "Hi _____, Please let me know you saw my message from [day of the week]. It would be great to connect and talk further. Thanks."

How to network with someone after he/she accepts your connection

If you make the initial outreach but don't know the person, consider a message like the one below after the person agrees to connect.

Subject line: [depends on the nature of your message but a general way to snag someone's attention: "Hope to learn more about your career" or "Could use your advice" — those two approaches make others feel important]

Hi _____,

I'm [first and last name], a [job title] at [name of company if you're employed] in [city]. Nice to meet you.

Thanks for accepting my connection request. I enjoyed learning more about your career, especially [one tidbit you find interesting and a question about it; for instance, "how you started your law firm's intellectual property division. Was it difficult to convince the firm to move into the digital space?"].

I'm not sure if you looked over my profile, but you might be interested in my [what you want the person to know; for instance, "own efforts with legal issues in the tech sector. Here's a quick example of my work: add URL here"].

[Then, what do you want from the other person? Perhaps you can use a line like, "I'm in the job market and would like to pick your brain about opportunities to apply my legal expertise. Would you have time for a quick phone call?"]

> NOTE: In this case, I put the "ask" (a phone call) at the bottom because the message flows better if you first explain why you find the person's career notable. You need to clarify why you chose to connect in the first place.

Please let me know what's possible.

Thanks,

– Your first and last name

Deeper Insight

Since you initiated the relationship with the invitation to connect, don't be too aggressive with the follow-up message. Start with proof you explored the other person's career and finish with a call to action (phone call, meeting, etc...). If you receive no answer, refer to the "Deeper Insight" on page 161.

How to ask someone to give you a recommendation

What makes a great LinkedIn recommendation? Stories, stories, stories. Tell the person to skip all the empty rhetoric about how "amazing" you are. Rely on your experiences.

Subject: Help with a recommendation

Hi _____,

I hope you're doing well. [A quick line to make conversation; for instance, "Did you clean off all the muck from the 10K mud run yet?"]

I'd like to add a recommendation to my LinkedIn profile about [how the person would praise you; for instance, "our company's role as the caterer for the mud run"]. Can you write a recommendation for me? It can be brief like three or four sentences.

[If you and the person share a memorable story that makes you look good, ask the person to write about it. For instance, "If you want, you can write about how our catering team never lost a step even when all 1,000 racers descended on the food tent at one time."]

> NOTE: Direct the person towards a fitting story. He/she might pick another but at least you offered an example to make it easier.

If you can write the recommendation, I'll send you a LinkedIn message with the request. I'm also happy to write one for you.

> NOTE: Ask first for the recommendation and then send over the actual request through LinkedIn.

Please let me know and thanks in advance,

– Your first name

Deeper Insight

Ask if the person would also like a recommendation on his/her profile and return the favor. And once the person does write a recommendation, be sure to send another LinkedIn message to say thanks.

How to write someone you met through a LinkedIn group

If you encounter someone interesting in a LinkedIn group or through a mutual friend/colleague, send an invitation to connect. If the person complies, follow up with a message to become better acquainted.

Subject line: Hope to connect, [then one of two lines]:

1. saw you in the [name of LinkedIn group]

2. friend/colleague of [name of person who links the two of you]

Hi _____,

I'm [first and last name], a [job title] at [name of company if you're employed] in [city]. Nice to meet you.

Thanks for accepting my connection request. I enjoyed learning more about your career, especially [one tidbit you find interesting and a question about it; for instance, "how you developed an online education tool to teach English as a second language. Did the idea come from a personal experience?"].

I'm not sure if you looked over my profile, but you might be interested in [what you want the person to know; for instance, "my time with app development in the educational space. Here's a quick example of my work: add URL here"].

NOTE: Reason #347 why you need a blog or portfolio. There are so many opportunities in networking correspondence to link people to your work so they can see what you're about.

164

[Then, what do you want from the other person? For instance, "I'd like to see if there are ways we can collaborate on an app I currently work on. Would you have time for a quick phone call? Please let me know."]

> NOTE: Once again, I put the "ask" (a phone call) at the bottom because the message flows better if you first explain why you find the person's career notable. You need to clarify why you chose to connect in the first place.

Thanks,

– Your first and last name

Deeper Insight

Don't overthink the networking game. If you find someone who could become a useful contact, send the message and see what comes back.

If you don't receive an answer after 48 hours, send a short follow up like, "Hi _____, Please let me know you saw my message from [day of the week]. It would be great to connect and talk further. Thanks."

LinkedIn Profile

HOW TO WRITE A STRONG PROFILE SUMMARY

You have 30 seconds to describe yourself. Can you do it?

With a LinkedIn summary, that's all the time you have. Sorry, no one wants to read your entire work history. Not even a little bit.

The summary section requires brevity and critical thinking. You must explain what you're about and the impact you make on others.

Let's begin with step 1, and you'll see what I mean.

Step 1: Who are you, really?

Keep it basic. In a nutshell, what are you known for? What's your identity? And how does your work help other people?

It's a useful exercise to describe yourself in less than ten seconds. Plus, it's important to think hard about the value you add to the market.

Here's an example for a young guy we'll call "Lamar."

"Every day, I protect sensitive information on thousands of people from hackers and cyberattacks."

At Lamar's professional core, that's the work he does AND how his work improves the lives of other people.

Step 2: What do you do?

Now take the opening line a bit deeper, but remember the 30-second rule. This is no time to delve into three huge paragraphs on everything you've done. Keep it rolling with specific details, like:

- ▸ Your title and company
- ▸ BRIEFLY what you do at the job
- ▸ Again, how your job *helps* people
- ▸ Specialties or areas of expertise if you need to describe your role a bit further

"As an information security analyst at Acme Hospital System in Sacramento, I manage the day-to-day flow of information into and out of five hospitals and two emergency centers. With a focus on database management, my job ensures critical computer systems, medical files and patient history remain active and never fail. My team and I stay updated on the latest trends in information security to not only keep Acme Hospital System safe but also on the cutting edge."

Step 3: Bring 'em home

In the final step, put a stamp on your LinkedIn summary.

By now the reader knows who you are and what you do. Now, finish out with a strong "closer" sentence.

Similar to your opening line, what's your mission as a working professional? What are you passionate about? And I know I'm a broken record but…how does your passion help other people?

Reiterate that point at the end, add a period and you're done.

Lamar's closing line:

"A hospital never sleeps, and the same goes for IT. If everything runs smoothly and nothing suffers a glitch, then I know I did my job."

Lamar's Full LinkedIn Profile Summary

Every day, I protect sensitive information on thousands of people from hackers and cyberattacks.

As an information security analyst at Acme Hospital System in Sacramento, I manage the day-to-day flow of information into and out of five hospitals and two emergency centers. With a focus on database management, my job ensures critical computer systems, medical files and patient history remain active and never fail. My team and I stay updated on the latest trends in information security to not only keep Acme Hospital System safe but also on the cutting edge.

A hospital never sleeps, and the same goes for IT. If everything runs smoothly and nothing suffers a glitch, then I know I did my job.

––––––

Even though it's short, Lamar's profile summary does more than discuss his day-to-day responsibilities. The summary explains his job, showcases his personality and proves why his work makes other people better.

In a vast ocean of online profiles, Lamar has a bio you will remember. And that's the goal: to be unforgettable.

Profile summaries for college students, recent grads and the unemployed

A LinkedIn profile summary should adjust with your career and position your skills and experience in different ways. It all depends on the scenario.

In the examples below, we'll use "Lamar" once again, our guy from the LinkedIn profile summary in the previous section. Remember, Lamar works in information security for a large hospital system so his various profile summaries will reflect his interest in computers and technology. Own who you are and *where* you are in your career.

College student

Step 1: Who are you, really?

I'm a junior at Big State University who majors in computer science and minors in mathematics.

> NOTE: Note how the major and minor are not capitalized as we discuss on page 35.

Step 2: What do you do?

You might say I'm a "tech geek" because I spend a lot time in the school's computer lab. That's where we learn to deconstruct laptops and build them back together. I'm vice president of the Campus Computer Club (CCC) and love to pick apart a motherboard or hard drive and help people with their computer challenges.

Step 3: Bring 'em home

When I graduate, I hope to find a job that uses computers and the latest technology to make the world a smarter place.

Deeper Insight

Lamar tells us he's passionate about computers, demonstrates his commitment (vice president of computer club) and discusses how he wants to use his tech skills to improve the world. Again, in the profile summary you must explain how your passion will help other people.

Recent grad

Step 1: Who are you, really?

I'm a recent computer science graduate from Big State University who wants to help a company make an impact through the use of new technology.

NOTE: Your goal is to make the company better. Don't worry — if the company succeeds, you will too.

Step 2: What do you do?

You might say I'm a "tech geek" because in college I was vice president of the Campus Computer Club (CCC) and spent a lot of time in the school's computer lab. I love to pick apart a motherboard or hard drive and help people with their computer challenges.

Step 3: Bring 'em home

Hackers, cyberattacks and other security issues are a reality today for companies big and small. I want to help a business not only stay protected but also grow and remain on the cutting edge.

Deeper Insight

Now that he needs a job, Lamar uses the profile summary to transition from college to the real world. He references his college credentials (vice president of computer club) and explains why his skills can benefit other people ("help a business…remain on the cutting edge").

What's your passion, and how can it help others?

Unemployed

Step 1: Who are you, really?

I am an information security analyst who provided IT support for three years for a large hospital system in Northern California.

Step 2: What do you do?

My specialties include installing firewalls, database management, implementing network disaster recovery plans and training teams on information security procedures — including people with limited knowledge of computers. By that I mean I can put "tech talk" in layman's terms.

169

NOTE: Be specific and technical when you list your skills. Don't write you're a "dedicated" professional. Skip the adjectives and tell people what services you provide ("installing firewalls").

Step 3: Bring 'em home

Computers and new technology are my passion. I stay updated on the latest information security software, protocols and best practices and understand the importance of a vigilant 24/7 security system for companies big and small.

"IT" is what I know and do best. I am ready for the next opportunity to apply my skills.

Deeper Insight

The hospital system, sadly, came under new management, and Lamar lost his job in the transition. Unemployed, his profile summary must adjust. This time, Lamar doesn't dwell on unemployment and instead focuses on his strengths. He mentions specific skills in case a recruiter, employer or robot scanner searches for someone with, for instance, "database management" ability.

Lamar also explains why information security — in other words, protecting someone's sensitive information — is his passion. He gives the reader a glimpse at his personality, which makes him more human, interesting and approachable. Sure, he's out of a job and that's rough. But the profile summary beams with confidence and energy, and that's attractive to an employer.

How to write about your work experience

In my view, LinkedIn work experience should look the same as resume work experience.

In both places, quantify your efforts, demonstrate success and highlight your specific skills as well as the tools and software you know how to use.

For a tutorial, turn to pages 209–215.

How to ask a recruiter to review your LinkedIn profile and make suggestions

Want to kill two birds with one stone? Ask a recruiter in your industry for ways to improve your profile. Then you may boost your career twice over:

1. The recruiter could offer great suggestions to sharpen your profile.

2. The recruiter may also take a closer look at you in reference to available jobs.

What if you land a job because you ask an expert how to sell yourself better? Crazier things have happened.

Subject line: Could use your advice on my LinkedIn profile

Hi Mr./Ms. _____[keep it formal],

My name is [first and last name], and I'm a [job title] in [city/state].

I am in the job market and in search of positions in the [industry where you want to work or find a new job]. If you have a few moments, are you able to review my profile and tell me how it can improve?

I see [show how you recognize the person's expertise as a recruiter; for instance, "you've been a recruiter in the mobile tech industry for the past four years so I'm sure you can offer solid insight on what employers want to see"].

NOTE: Don't forget to stroke the ego.

If possible, I'd like you to tell me:

- If my profile summary clearly explains my experience and the value I provide

171

- Any key industry terms or phrases that recruiters and employers use to search for candidates

- If there's any experience I should highlight more than I do now

Please let me know what's possible. I know I would benefit from your perspective and knowledge.

Thanks,

– Your first and last name

Email signature

Deeper Insight

Don't ask for any job leads. All you want is advice right now. If the relationship develops, you might feel comfortable asking about job opportunities. But at the onset, you should stick to the "help me improve" route.

Chapter 6
Handwritten Notes

The Essentials

THE GENERAL RULES OF A PROPER LETTER

How to send a handwritten note:

- If the note opens vertically, write on the bottom half. Horizontally, write on the right side.
- Put the day's date (month and day as in "3/27" or "March 27") in the upper right.
- Address the person by name in the upper left.
- Take your time and make sure each word is legible.
- Consider writing the note first on your computer to make all necessary edits. Once you have a final draft, transfer the words to paper and pen. That way, you only need to write the note once in case you don't like how it sounds or you make a mistake.
- Use blue or black pen. Other colors may look unprofessional.
- Estimate the length of the letter so your words are large (or small) enough to fill the entire space.
- Write the address legibly on the envelope so the USPS can deliver the note without any trouble.

Why and when to send a handwritten note

Yes, handwritten notes are tedious, require postage and hurt your wrist. But think about it this way: fewer and fewer people write thank-you notes today, which makes the ones you compose ten times more valuable than they once were.

You write a handwritten note...

- ▸ When someone does something extra special for your career
- ▸ When someone gives generously of his/her time to help you
- ▸ When you want to solidify or strengthen a relationship
- ▸ When you feel an email isn't enough

Here's the deal: there's no wrong time to send a handwritten note. If you have a few moments (and an envelope and stamp), stick a letter in the mail.

> NOTE: Better yet, have a few notes, stamps and envelopes at your desk so you're ready when a thank-you opportunity arises.

It's unlikely the person will respond to your message with "Thanks, how nice!" but you can trust he/she will appreciate the note, save it and think of you in a whole new light.

Plus, the act of sending a letter will make you feel great too.

How to thank someone after a networking meeting

Month/Day

Name,

Thank you again for meeting with me (earlier today/ yesterday). I took a lot from our conversation, especially (be specific; for instance, "your insight into the engineering business. Plus, thanks for connecting me with your friend at Acme Corporation. That's a huge help"). Please let me know if I can ever return the favor with your career. I'm happy to lend a hand. Have a great week,

Your first name

Deeper Insight

Reference your conversation and be specific ("insight into the engineering business") and also offer to return the favor.

The thank-you note should go out within 48 hours of the conversation.

How to thank someone after a job interview

Month/Day

Name,

Thank you again for the time (earlier today/yesterday). As I said, I'm interested in the position and would like to be part of your team. I especially enjoyed hearing about (reference a moment from the conversation; for instance, "the company's push for more eco-friendly products. That's a great initiative and will certainly pay off").

Please let me know if I can answer any further questions.

Thanks again, and I hope to hear from you.

Your first name

Deeper Insight

Reference your conversation and be specific ("the company's push for more eco-friendly products").

The thank-you note should go out within 48 hours of the conversation.

How to thank someone who went above and beyond

Month/Day

Name,

Thank you for (what the person did for you; for instance, "handling my shift while I was out sick with the flu. You came through HUGE for me"). I appreciate your help so much and (quick example of what the help let you do; for instance, "I didn't fall behind on my follow-ups with the Georgia clients"). Please let me know how I can help you in the future. I'm more than happy to lend a hand. Thanks again!

Your first name

Deeper Insight

Make sure to remind the person how he/she helped you ("handling my shift while I was out sick with the flu"). Also offer to return the favor.

The thank-you note should go out within 48 hours.

Chapter 7
Graduate School Templates

Basics for Back to School

HOW TO CONTACT A FACULTY MEMBER BEFORE YOU APPLY TO THE PROGRAM

The graduate school email below helps in two ways:

1. Allows you to learn more about the graduate program

2. Develops a relationship with a faculty member, which could prove useful during the application process

---

Subject line: Interested to learn more about [name of program] at [name of school]

Hi [Professor/Dean _____],

My name is [first and last name], and I am interested in the [name of program; for instance, "criminology program"] at the [name of college/university].

[Give the person your short bio; for instance, "I am a sales associate for a large farm supply company but feel I want to make a career change and focus on criminology."]

[Then explain how you researched the graduate program and the person you're writing; for instance, "Big State University has a well-regarded criminology program, and I see you personally have published a lot of important work in the field, including a 2012 study on the effects of an increased police presence in suburban communities. I'm also interested in the impact of police on society, and I appreciate the research you conducted."]

> NOTE: Link to the person's work (2012 study) when possible.

I'd like to learn more about the [subject; for instance, "criminology"] program and what life is like as a student. Are you available for a phone call? Please let me know.

> NOTE: Don't ask questions about the application process. Instead, focus on learning more about the graduate program and the faculty member's career.

[Or, if you expect to visit the campus, ask, "I plan to be on campus in the coming weeks. Do you have a few minutes to meet with me and answer questions?"]

Thanks, and I hope to hear from you.

– Your first name

Email signature

Deeper Insight

In the email, you show interest in the school, the graduate field of study AND the professor's own work. It's not brown-nosing — it's about building a relationship.

If you can visit the campus, ask to meet in person. A physical introduction is much more effective than email or phone. Before you meet, make sure you understand the faculty person's research and courses he/she teaches. You will impress the person with how much you know.

How to contact a faculty member while you're in school to learn about his/her work

As a graduate student, you should continue to nurture relationships with faculty members. The email below lets you make introductions and explore the chance to work alongside or under someone new.

Subject line: Interested to learn more about your work on [type of research]

Hi [Professor/Dean _____],

My name is [first and last name], and I am a graduate student in the [name of program within your college/university]. I am working on my [master's/PhD] and expect to finish in [graduation date].

As I pursue my degree in [name of degree], I would like to learn more about your own research on [what the person studies; for instance, "climate change in the Mississippi River Delta"].

NOTE: Link to the person's work (climate change study) when possible.

[Then explain why you find the research interesting; for instance, "I am curious about your research methods as they could help my own efforts on a climate project over the summer."]

179

Is there a time I can stop by your office and talk for a few minutes? Please let me know your schedule when you have a chance.

Thanks,

– Your first name

Email signature

Deeper Insight

Ask for a face-to-face meeting rather than an email exchange or phone call. You will create a more meaningful relationship if you meet in person. Plus, if you're both on the same campus, it shouldn't be too hard to connect.

How to contact a current student before you apply to the program

Who better to give you the "inside scoop" on a graduate program than a current student? Send an email and gather the details from someone already enrolled.

Subject line: Interested to learn more about [name of program] at [name of school]

Hi _____,

My name is [first and last name], and I am interested in the [name of program; for instance, "John Doe College of Business"] at the [name of school; for instance, "Big State University"].

[Give the person your short bio; for instance, "I am a junior investment manager at a large financial firm, and I'd like to pursue an MBA while I stay at my job."]

[Then explain what you want; for instance, "I see you're a student at Big State, and I'd like to pick your brain about the program. Any insight you can offer would be helpful."]

> NOTE: How do you find students to contact? Check out the graduate program website and look for students' names in articles, blogs or photo captions. Then track the person down via LinkedIn. If you meet a graduate student at a networking event, happy hour or through friends, ask for the person's email address and/or business card.

Please let me know if you're free to talk by phone over the next week.

> NOTE: If you live in the same general area, you can also ask for an in-person meeting. Even if the person doesn't have a role in the admissions process, relationships will be crucial once you're on campus.

Thanks,

– Your first name

Email signature

Deeper Insight

Be polite, ask for a quick phone call and be flexible with the other person's schedule. And as you would for an employer, investigate the student's own research projects or fields of interest. It will make the person feel you value his/her time.

How to network among classmates

While you're in school, don't forget to network with classmates. Lean on each other to not only collaborate on projects (and cry on each other's shoulders during exam weeks) but also position yourself for opportunities upon graduation.

Subject line: Fellow grad student at [name of school], hope to [collaborate/network]

Hi _____,

My name is [first and last name], and I am a graduate student in the [name of school]. I am working on my [master's/PhD] and expect to finish [graduation date].

> NOTE: Fully explain your degree program, field of study and year of graduation.

[Then, explain what you want from the person. If you'd like to work together, write a sentence like, "I'm writing to explore ways we can collaborate since we both work on similar environmental research projects. I read your study on declining snowfall and its ecological impact, and I think there's synergy with my own work on the decrease in wildlife."]

Would you want to get together and discuss ways to collaborate?

Let me know a time and place that could work for you.

Thanks, and I hope to hear from you.

– Your first name

Email signature

Deeper Insight

Use your time IN school to develop a network once you're OUT of school. We're only as strong as the relationships we build and maintain.

How to ask a professor for a letter of recommendation

A former professor is a terrific person to vouch for you in a graduate school application. The professor has seen you in the classroom at the undergraduate level and knows the kind of student you would be at the graduate level.

Subject line: Letter of recommendation for graduate school

Hi _____,

I hope you're doing well.

[Ask a question specific to the person's career; for instance, "How is everything going at Big State University? How are your students this semester?"]

I plan to apply for [tell the person what you're up to; for instance, "a master's in library science at Tech University"] and hope to go back to school [ex: this fall, this spring, next fall, etc...].

> NOTE: Explain the exact graduate program instead of a line like, "I hope to attend graduate school at Tech University."

Would you be able to write a letter of recommendation for me? If so, I think the [college/university] faculty would like to know about the time [your story; for instance, "I came to class one hour early to prepare for our big group presentation on Big State's architectural history and then led the discussion for our four-person team"].

The recommendation doesn't need to be long. A couple of paragraphs is fine, and I hope the specific story will make me stand out.

NOTE: Let the professor know he/she doesn't need to write 1,000 words. Short and sweet will do.

Thanks so much,

– Your first name

Email signature

Deeper Insight

Notice how you GIVE the person a story to tell about you (if you have one available). Provide details to jog the person's memory and explain why you want the reference letter to include the story (it will "make me stand out").

Then, allow the person 48 hours to respond in case you need to follow up with, "I want to make sure you saw my email the other day about a recommendation letter. Please let me know and thanks!"

If you can't think of a memorable story, then ask the person to be specific as he/she describes you. A letter that reads "she was one of the best students I ever had" — but then never backs up the claim — will do you little good.

How to ask an employer or former employer for a letter of recommendation

Like an email from a professor, you want the employer to explain WHY you're "driven" and "dedicated" through a meaningful story. So ask for one.

Subject line: Letter of recommendation for graduate school

Hi _____,

I hope you're doing well.

[Ask a question specific to the person's career; for instance, "How is everything going at the high school? Do you have fun kids this year?"]

I am applying for [your situation; for instance, "a master's of music education at Big State University"] and hope to go back to school [ex: this fall, this spring, next fall, etc...or as a part-time student while I continue to work at _____].

> NOTE: Explain the exact graduate program instead of a line like, "I hope to attend graduate school at Big State University."

Would you be able to write a letter of recommendation for me? If so, I think the [college/university] faculty would like to know about the time [your story; for instance, "I was your substitute teacher when you were on maternity leave and organized the spring musical production in your place. That's a solid example of my ability to take charge and show passion for music in schools"].

The recommendation doesn't need to be long. A couple of paragraphs is fine, and I hope a specific story will make me stand out.

Thanks so much,

– Your first name

Email signature

Deeper Insight

For more, refer to the "Deeper Insight" on page 184.

How to thank a professor or employer for a letter of recommendation

If a professor or employer takes the time to write a letter of recommendation, you'd better come right back with a heartfelt thank-you note. Do not take the relationship and assistance for granted.

Subject line: Thank you for the letter of recommendation

Hi _____,

Thank you again for the letter of recommendation as I apply for [degree program at college/university].

If you saw the letter of recommendation:

Your letter is perfect and struck the right tone about my interest in [field of study]. I like how you mention I [give one example that stands out; for instance, "took charge on our group assignment about mobile apps and attention span when it was clear we needed better direction. I think the admissions department at _____ will appreciate the example"].

> NOTE: If the person worked hard on the letter, then he/she is proud of it. That's why you should make special note of why YOU find it special too.

If the person sent the letter directly to the graduate school and you never saw it:

I have no doubt you did a great job with the letter and placed me in a favorable light.

The rest of the email — both versions:

Please let me know if there's ever a way I can return the favor.

Thanks, and I'll be sure to let you know if I am accepted into the program at [name of college/university].

> NOTE: Do not forget to tell the person if you're accepted. Keep your network informed.

Have a great day,

– Your first name

Email signature

Deeper Insight

Significant favors — like a letter of recommendation — are tough to come by. It's critical you thank the person after he/she writes the letter. Don't wait on the thank-you note and make the person think, "Gee, a thank-you note would have been nice."

Have paper, pen and a stamp handy? Send a handwritten note instead.

Chapter 8
Phone Conversations

How to Talk the Talk

NINE TIMES YOU SHOULD PICK UP THE PHONE INSTEAD OF SEND AN EMAIL

Yes, it's easier to fire off an email than make a phone call. On the phone we're put "on the spot" and need to come across polished and professional. It's more stressful and requires more effort.

Still, there are times when a phone call isn't preferred but necessary. Why? On the phone, you handle your business more quickly and show you're not afraid to talk with someone in real time.

Consider the scenarios below as you decide: email or phone?

You should pick up the phone when...

1. You send an email with critical information and the person doesn't respond within ten minutes. It's time to call and check on whether the email came through.

2. You have a lot of information to pass along, and it's easier to discuss over the phone than write a huge email.

3. You want to have a conversation with someone rather than a back-and-forth email chain.

4. You have a request or need information from someone, and it's faster to call than send an email and wait for a response.

5. You send two or more emails to the same person (about the same topic) but never receive a response.

6. You send an email to ask about internship opportunities but never receive a response.

7. You send an email about a networking opportunity and then another email if the person doesn't respond. If you receive no answer after email #2, and it's someone you need to meet, then it's time to call.

8. You've held a back-and-forth email conversation with someone but never spoken. If you want to take the relationship further, you must hold an actual conversation.

How to introduce yourself properly

YOU: Hi, I'm [first and last name], and I am calling about _____.

Two points about the intro:

▶ Don't say, "*This is* _____, and I am calling about _____." You're not a "this." You're a person. Go with, "I'm _____" or "My name is _____."

▶ Don't forget to introduce yourself. State your name *clearly* before you ask for someone or something. The introduction shows maturity.

How to make the other person feel important

Remember, you need to give before you get so take an interest in other people. Pore over the details of their lives. You'll have your chance to speak soon enough.

Let's say you're on a networking phone call.

Ask questions like:

- Tell me more about you. What kind of work do you do at [name of company]?
- What do you enjoy the most about the job?
- What's a typical day like for you?
- Where do you see opportunity for your business?

And don't forget to:

- Thank the person at the beginning and end of the conversation for speaking with you.
- Ask if there are any ways you can help the other person.
- Offer to send over your resume or portfolio examples in case the person will connect you to someone else.

How to ask about internship opportunities

YOU: Hi, my name is _____, and I am calling to find out if your company has any internship opportunities for the [spring semester/fall semester/coming year]. I'm a [ex: freshman] at [name of college/university] and I'm majoring in [your major].

Are you the right person to talk to or should I speak with someone else?

Then, if you do locate the right person, make sure you take down his/her name, ask how to spell it and then use the exact name as you address the internship application/future emails.

A phone call like the one above allows you to form a relationship (a small one) with the person who chooses interns. When you address the person by name in the application, it cements how the two of you "know each other." The connection can help if the person decides between ten applicants but only "knows" one of them: you.

How to make sure the company received your job application

YOU: Hi, my name is _____, and [earlier this week/last week] I applied for the position of _____. I am calling to make sure you received my application.

Are you the right person to talk to or should I speak with someone else?

If you locate the right person, keep the conversation brief and don't use the call to elaborate on your professional bio. If the person opens the door a bit and tosses out small talk like, "Yes…I see your application here. So you went to Big State? Oh, my brother went there…," then you can talk a bit about your college and career. But again, don't abuse the conversation or the person's time.

Speak when spoken to. Otherwise, your objective is to confirm the company received your application.

Thank the person by name ("Thanks, Karen. I appreciate it.") and wrap up the call. Your job here is done.

NOTE: More on the power of name dropping on page 24.

How to prepare for an interview (phone, Skype or Google+ Hangout)

Before you dial the number, have this info ready:

▸ Two to three highlights from your resume the employer would find relevant. What have you done to prepare for the job you want? Study the job description closely and explain how you have already exemplified the kind of "hard" skills the company seeks.

> *NOTE: What do I mean by "hard" skills? Tangible work experience as well as the use of software and tools the company values. Don't tell the employer you're a "hard worker" without facts and figures to back up the claim.*

▸ Three stories about your work experience to demonstrate you're right for the job (more on the storytelling strategy for job interviews on page 203).

▸ One or two examples of recent projects from the company website to prove you did your research.

- One or two questions about those recent projects (ex: "I see you do a lot of marketing campaigns with healthcare companies. Do you feel there's an opportunity for your team in the healthcare space?").

- How can you help the company make more money? What's your value-add? Have one or two ideas ready (ex: "I have solid experience selling products online and my e-commerce skills will help the company expand its offerings on the website").

- Finally, stand up when you're on the phone. It makes breathing easier, which improves the strength and quality of your voice.

Chapter 9
The Power of Stories

Cover Letters

WHY YOU SHOULD TELL STORIES IN COVER LETTERS

"Hi, my name is _____, and I am interested in the position of _____"...

Guess what the employer thinks?

"I've seen this same cover letter about 1,000 times. Next!"

So let's try something new...

Instead of a predictable opening line, lead with a compelling personal story. If the anecdote relates directly to the job description — and the skills it requires — you stand a much greater chance the employer will be impressed with your application.

In other words: a stronger cover letter might get you hired.

Why do we read books? Go to the movies? Watch TV dramas?

Because we love stories. They move us, inspire us, transport us and above all... they entertain us. Why should a cover letter be a flat, unemotional document? Who decided it should exist only to regurgitate the information on a resume or to fill up five bloated paragraphs with everything you've done so far in your career?

No one decided those rules yet we slowly came to accept them.

On the following pages, I will show you how to write your own story in the first paragraph of a cover letter for any job. I provide the general outline for the story-telling strategy and two complete cover letters.

There are three advantages to the storytelling style:

- They catch the reader's attention immediately.

- They demonstrate your ability to do the job in question.

- They leave a lasting impression.

Every one of us has skills and knowledge employers crave — even from an internship, as a volunteer or in college. Usually, though, we don't convey how our experiences make us strong job candidates. If you learn to harness the power of your stories, it may open new doors for your career.

Outline for the storytelling cover letter

An effective storytelling cover letter contains the six parts listed below. In the two examples on the following pages, I point out where each part occurs within the letter.

PART 1: Open with a line that places readers into the story. Grab their attention and make them think, "Hmm, this is different. I want to know more."

PART 2: Include concrete details about the story. The more specific you are, the more colorful the anecdote. Provide hard numbers when appropriate and give exact locations and job titles.

PART 3: Demonstrate how the story applies to the job you want. Refer to the job description and make sure the anecdote reflects the person the company wants to hire.

PART 4: Show you researched the company and understand its opportunities in the broader marketplace. Also explain how you will help the company grow its business. Ultimately, managers want to know how you will make the company more successful.

PART 5: Share more of your qualities as they relate to the story at the top. Again, reference the job description, touch on qualities you know the company admires and show how you would be a good cultural fit.

PART 6: Mention your story one final time and bring the cover letter full circle.

Cover letter example if you're a recent grad

The job: Entry-level program associate at a nonprofit. Duties include research, event planning and assisting senior-level managers. Company wants a person who:

- ▸ Works well on a team
- ▸ Knows how to take charge and be a leader
- ▸ Can multitask and handle stressful situations
- ▸ Is easygoing but a hard worker
- ▸ Brings creative ideas to the table and can help the company grow

---

First and Last Name

Email: xxxxx@gmail.com ▪ **Mobile**: 555-555-5555 ▪ **Address**: Street, City, State, Zip

LinkedIn URL ▪ #yournameportfolio (*what's this? go to page 50*)

First and Last Name of the Employer
Job Title
Company
Street Address
City, State, Zip

["Dear Mr./Ms. _____" or "Dear Hiring Professional" if you can't find the right person],

PART 1   I looked up at the sky and couldn't believe it: storm clouds.

PART 2   For months, my team and I had prepared for the annual Big Nonprofit Association charity bash, in which students throw a party for 24 hours straight and raise money for children's hospitals. We had the campus quad reserved and the event ready to go. Then, out of nowhere, a huge thunderstorm threatened to ruin everything.

As team leader, I organized our group to take the dance party inside the gymnasium, notified all participants about the location change and worked with an audio/visual tech to ensure the music played indoors. Within three hours, we had the Big Nonprofit Association party back on track and, in the end, collected $11,000 for charity, the most we had ever raised.

PART 3   My name is Jennifer Sutherland, and I want to be your next program associate. I know it can be challenging to organize, plan and execute big events, and I am ready to work hard for the [name of organization]. Issues and setbacks can appear without warning, and it takes determination to work through them.

PART 4 As I researched your organization, I learned a great deal about the inspiring work you do with the Little Nonprofit Association and its annual fundraising walk that supports cancer research. I also read about challenges in the nonprofit sector. For people to donate today, it's essential to reach them in meaningful ways, particularly online. I have experience building community and generating buzz on social networks and would do my best to bring fresh thinking to the table.

PART 5 Above all, I am excited to take my hands-on skills in social media and event planning and put them to use for your organization. I enjoy being part of a group, know how to multitask and always finish what I start. I also try to be curious and would want to learn as much as I can from your team.

PART 6 The Big Nonprofit Association party taught me the importance of quick decisions and staying focused in a hectic situation. I am ready to bring the same work ethic and energy to your organization.

Thanks so much, and I hope to hear from you soon.

– Your first and last name

Deeper Insight

If you're a recent grad, you don't need actual job experience to impress an employer. Think back on your college years, internships and part-time jobs and share a story to prove your ability. **Let the story do the selling.**

Cover letter example if you have work experience

The job: Sales executive for an educational software company. The company wants a person who:

▸ Has two to three years of experience in a sales position
▸ Is a self-starter and knows how to take charge

▸ Is comfortable working independently or on a team

▸ Can think creatively, find innovative solutions and help the company grow

———

First and Last Name

Email: xxxxx@gmail.com ▪ **Mobile**: 555-555-5555 ▪ **Address**: Street, City, State, Zip

LinkedIn URL ▪ #yournameportfolio (*what's this? go to page 50*)

First and Last Name of the Employer
Job Title
Company
Street Address
City, State, Zip

["Dear Mr./Ms. _____" or "Dear Hiring Professional" if you can't find the right person],

PART 1   Jim Robisky said "No" to me so many times, I lost count.

As a sales rep for a mid-size IT firm, I tried time and again to convince Robisky, the VP of technology for a large hospital system, he needed to upgrade all of his servers and begin to move much of the hospital's data onto the "cloud." Phone calls, handwritten notes, drop-in visits — nothing seemed to work.

PART 2   Then, I took a different approach. I knew Robisky typically attends a monthly networking event at the chamber of commerce. I also expected another client of ours — who has fully embraced the "cloud" — to be at the event too. When I saw both people in the room, a co-worker and I introduced the two, mentioned the benefits of cloud computing and let my client sing its praises to Robisky.

A few moments later, Robisky turned to me and said, "Call my office on Monday. I think I'm ready to explore the cloud a bit more."

PART 3   Six months later, the hospital system remains our biggest client. My name is Stephen Hirsch, and I want to be your next sales executive. I know sales is a tough game, but I enjoy the chance to win over even the most stubborn prospect.

PART 4   As I read about your company, I learned a lot about the software you've developed (ex: PlayTime card game) and how it can make a real impact on school-age children. Through my research, I also understand the educational software landscape is highly competitive. It takes a combination of great products and a committed sales team to find continued success.

PART 5   Above all, I want to apply my sales experience in a meaningful way and would enjoy helping children develop math and reading skills from an early age. I also like to collaborate with other team members, craft smart sales and marketing strategies and work alongside people who are passionate about early education.

PART 6   The Jim Robisky experience proved, with enough grit and creativity, I can make the deal happen. I would love the chance to bring my skillset and work ethic to your team.

Thanks so much, and I hope to hear from you soon.

– Your first and last name

Deeper Insight

You have work experience. Terrific. Use it as a marketing tool and demonstrate HOW you're right for the job.

Stephen Hirsch's story is much more effective than if he claims he's a determined sales exec. The Jim Robisky story **proves** it.

Also, notice how the job description asks for a person who can work solo and on a team. In the story, I mention Hirsch approaches Robisky at the networking event *with a coworker*. It's a subtle piece of information but shows Hirsch is a team player.

As much as possible, your cover letter should reflect the person the company wants. Read the job description closely and sprinkle in details that make you appealing and, all along, underscore how you will make the business more successful.

More Storytelling Opportunities

REFERENCE LETTERS

Like the letter of recommendation on page 132, a short story about success on the job will go a long way with an employer. *Subject line can be: Help with a reference letter*

The template:

> Hi _____,
>
> Hope you're doing well. [Ask a question about the other person's world; for instance, "How is everything going during tax season? Are you staying sane?"]
>
> I have applied for [explain what you're up to; for instance, "a job at Acme Corporation as a junior investment banker"], and the company asked for a reference letter. Are you able to write one for me?
>
> In your letter, it would be great if you reference a situation where I demonstrated my work ethic. The more specific, the better. For instance, you can write about the time I [be specific; for instance, "stayed at work until 11 pm to make sure we finished the project in time for the big presentation the next morning"].
>
> The letter doesn't need to be long. A couple of paragraphs will do.
>
> Please let me know, and thanks a lot.
>
> – Your first name
>
> Email signature

Deeper Insight

Not only will employers *read* the "short story" reference letter — as opposed to skimming a boring one in five seconds — but it also might push your application to the top. Remember: the other job seekers provided flavorless, colorless recommendations.

You jump off the page with a career snapshot that speaks volumes about your character.

Also make sure to send a thank-you note (email or handwritten) to the person for such a terrific reference letter.

If you can't think of a memorable story, then ask the person to be specific as he/she describes you. The more details, the better.

Job interviews

The next time you have a job interview, walk into the room with a pen, paper and a list of three bullet points.

The three bullets are quick reminders of success stories and ways to let your personality shine. That's because stories demonstrate in vivid detail why you are right for the job and how you can turn a typical Q&A interview into a dynamic, *memorable* conversation.

Stories already work great on cover letters (page 195) and recommendation letters (pages 183 and 184). Now they will help you nail a job interview.

Example: You want a job as a client manager at a tech firm. Let's up the stakes and say you're 25, spent the first three years of your career at a nonprofit and don't have experience in the private sector. It doesn't matter. Your stories can still carry you.

Before the interview, jot down three great stories from your life that show you know how to lead and solve problems. It can look like the list below.

My Three Stories

1. The fire alarm

2. The sick day

3. The camping trip

Then, as the interview goes along, look to weave the three stories into your answers. Many interview questions focus on ability or past work experience so you will have opportunities. **The key is to have storytelling as your go-to strategy from the start.**

In my example, I chose two stories from the workplace and one from someone's personal life. Now, the person may not use all three stories in an interview, but they remain on standby if the conversation allows.

#1: The Fire Alarm Incident

Question: Why are you interested in the project manager position at our firm?

Answer: I have spent the past three years at a nonprofit and gained a lot of great skills running different programs and events. I'm ready for a new challenge, and I prefer fast-paced environments like your company where I would need to think quickly. In fact, **let me tell you a good story.**

About six months ago, our nonprofit hosted its annual fundraising gala. Five hundred people, black tie affair, the whole nine yards. Right as we're about to announce our record-breaking donation total, the fire alarm goes off and won't stop blaring. Everyone's looking around for what to do so I jump on the microphone and calmly ask 500 PEOPLE to exit the banquet hall and go outside.

The fire department came, searched the place and didn't find anything. Then I herded all 500 people back into the room and kept the night on track. So I have definitely handled stressful situations and stayed calm when everything broke down. And I'll be poised again when a client has a critical challenge.

Boss thinks: OK, this person can certainly get through a rough day at work. Excellent.

#2: The Sick Day

Question: What's your greatest strength?

Answer: I think my greatest strength is I'm resourceful. Actually, **I have a great story about that too**. A year ago, half of our team at the nonprofit got sick with the flu. It's an eight-person team so we were down to four employees for an entire week. We also had a huge program the same weekend — a jump rope for health event with over 250 children.

With only four of us in the office, we had to use our time and energy wisely. I handled online sign-ups and coordinated with the caterer. I directed two of my co-workers to oversee the awards presentation and music. And our fourth co-worker was our intern, Kacie. I quickly taught Kacie how to work the phones and answer questions from parents and the media. We worked hard that week, but the four of us got it done and the jump rope event was a success. So I like to think I can rise to the challenge even with limited resources or staff...and not miss a beat.

Boss thinks: Wow, what a strong manager. Poised and everything.

#3: The Camping Trip

Question: What do you like to do outside of work?

Answer: I'm big into the outdoors. Last weekend, my friends and I went camping in Shenandoah National Park. It's actually **kind of a crazy story**. We set up our tent in what we thought was a remote part of the mountains. After an hour or so, this huge group of people showed up in Renaissance-era costumes. Apparently a local acting troupe is doing a Shakespeare play and came out to the wilderness to practice its lines. It was weird and also hilarious.

Boss thinks: Great stuff. Didn't expect to hear a story like that!

OK, let's recap

Do you see the power of stories? **You can't prove your ability unless you provide on-the-job examples.** And if the interviewer asks about your personal life, you have a story ready there too. Plenty of people like the outdoors, but no one else would ever talk about the acting troupe situation. It's yours and makes you different!

Well, hold on a second...

You might think, "What if there's no natural way to tell a story? Won't it sound awkward?"

Not so fast. You can answer a lot of common interview questions with a story:

▸ **Why should we hire you?**

"Well, let me give you a good example of my work performance..."

▸ **How do you deal with stressful situations?**

"Let me tell you about this one time..."

▸ **Is there a moment when you exercised leadership?**

"Yes, there was this one week when half of my office got the flu and..."

And finally...

The boss says, "Do you have any questions for me?"

That's when you go with the four questions everyone should ask in a job interview as found on page 221. Again, they show you're unlike every other person who asks typical fluff like, "How much vacation time will I have?"

Instead, you drop a gem like, "I see we can expect a huge growth in cloud-based services. What does the increase mean for the company and the services you provide?"

Chapter 10
Effective Resumes

The Fundamentals

HOW TO WRITE AN IMPRESSIVE OBJECTIVE STATEMENT

With an objective statement, our instinct is to dazzle employers with adjectives.

"Highly **motivated** professional with **excellent** leadership skills. **Performance-driven** individual who can create **immeasurable** success on a team and turn **complex** problems into solutions."

We think, "If I tell the manager I am 'motivated,' THAT'S going to set me apart. Nailed it."

Here's the deal: the boss has a stack of 50 resumes from people who ALL claim to be "motivated."

On a resume, adjectives don't make us stand out; they lump us in with everyone else.

As I explain with cover letters on page 195, don't tell employers you're "highly motivated." Show them with concrete examples. Rely on key details to craft an objective statement no one else can match.

Let's say "Dave" has three years of work experience in medical sales and wants a new job in the same field.

Old objective statement:

"Highly motivated professional with excellent customer service skills and a strong ability to turn complex problems into solutions. Accomplished sales leader with a track record of success."

Again, the issue: Dave's objective statement could appear on anyone's resume for any job. It's not specific to his career in medical sales and uses empty rhetoric ("accomplished sales leader"). Dave, don't TELL me you're "accomplished." SHOW me.

New objective statement:

"Experienced medical sales professional who provides surgical supplies to hospitals throughout Georgia and South Carolina; manage 18 accounts and in 2014 grew sales totals 22% to $1.3 million."

How many other people could write an objective statement like Dave? That's right. Zero. It's Dave's story and his alone.

Every time Dave could have been bland, he doubles down on the details.

- "Highly motivated professional" becomes "Experienced medical sales professional"
- "Excellent customer service skills" becomes "manage 18 accounts"
- "Complex problems into solutions" (the most cliche phrase EVER on a resume) becomes "grew sales totals 22 percent to $1.3 million"

If Dave's objective statement were a book title, it would fly off the shelf. His description is impressive from start to finish because it's 100 percent substance.

You might think, "OK, great for Dave. But I recently graduated and don't have work experience. What then, Mr. Writer Man?"

Now I'm going to change the tune on you.

If you don't have work experience, skip the objective statement. That's right — leave it out.

Until you have concrete results on the job, start the resume with your biggest selling point to date: your skills. List out software, tools, programs, trainings and certifications.

NOTE: Think hard about the skills section. Don't write how you are "Familiar with office phone systems." Instead, list the actual name of the phone system and the company that makes it. The details make your resume stronger.

Also, do not list Microsoft Office as a "skill." It's not impressive anymore. Everyone can use Word, Excel and PowerPoint.

Then below the "Skills" section, go into your experience.

Since you're at square one of your career, you don't need a passionate and finely-tuned "objective." You need to apply your skills at a job and start on your journey.

As long as you work hard at every opportunity, the objective will reveal itself in time.

How to make any job look remarkable

You might think your job is nothing special or, better yet, a stepping stone to an actual career. You figure, "Who wants to learn about my boring job? I should play up my work ethic and personality instead." So your resume is full of words like:

▶ hard worker
▶ team player
▶ dependable

Wrong. Plain wrong.

You can make any job, no matter how mundane, jump off the page. It all starts with one question: Where's the drama?

Every job has moments of stress or high emotion. Those are ideal opportunities to demonstrate HOW you're a hard worker, team player or dependable. Employers are like the rest of us: they want to be entertained.

Forget your job title or how "unimpressive" it might appear. Give people the drama.

Here's a Quick Example

Let's say "Shannon Jones" lands a job through a temp agency to file papers and answer phones at a medical practice. Maybe not the job she wants for 30 years, but it's what she has right now.

Typical work experience on her resume:

- ▸ Answer phones and provide customer service at a medical office
- ▸ Assist people with concerns in a friendly and courteous manner
- ▸ File patient paperwork and help to keep the office organized

Again, where's the drama? How can she add sizzle to an "ordinary" job? Revised work experience on her resume:

- ▸ Answer more than 75 phone calls a day at one of the busiest medical practices in Houston
- ▸ Check in 50–60 patients each day and often work with three to four people at a time
- ▸ Help to manage files for nearly 2,700 patients and digitize critical medical information

See what I mean? Do you feel the drama now?

The two job descriptions sound like different people. In the second version, I focus on hectic moments in the workday and include numbers to explain how much of everything.

Check in 50–60 patients each day and often work with three to four people at a time

That's far more interesting than:

Assist people with concerns in a friendly and courteous manner

Now the employer pictures the applicant hustling — and keeping order — in a crazy doctor's office. Cool under pressure, doesn't get rattled, handles the stress.

So…how do you add drama to YOUR resume?

Think about work experience like this: how are/were my jobs dramatic or at least challenging? What made them tense or stressful?

Then, bring those moments into your resume.

Replace the line:

▸ *Managed warehouse and handled ordering and restocking of supplies*

With:

▸ *Managed 17,000 sq. ft. warehouse and handled restocking of over 500 different supplies, which were shipped from 37 states and seven countries*

Which version do you find more appealing?

Yep. The employer does too.

Professional resume template

The one-page resume below is for a person with 3+ years of work experience in fundraising/development. You might be a recent grad or have more than two to three years of experience. That's fine. The lessons in the resume apply to any stage of a person's career.

Read the resume all the way through and then see the explanations for each section at the bottom.

Joseph Green

Email: xxxxx@gmail.com ▪ **Mobile**: 555-555-5555 ▪ **Address**: Street, City, State, Zip
LinkedIn URL ▪ #josephgreenportfolio

Experienced development professional who has managed three capital campaigns and organized volunteers to raise over $2.4 million in their own communities. Strong knowledge of online fundraising tools and effective team manager on projects and events.

SKILLS

▸ Proficient with fundraising websites Example 1, Example 2 and Example 3

▸ Oversee e-newsletter campaigns through the programs Example 1, Example 2 and Example 3

▸ Manage [name of content management system] websites and [name of social media platform] fan pages

211

▸ Organize large databases, conduct financial forecasting and monitor ongoing campaigns

EXPERIENCE

NON PROFIT A ▪ Washington, DC ▪ November 2012– Present
Associate Director of Development

▸ Part of an organization that raises more than $8 million annually for cancer research
▸ Grew organization's social media presence 400% over two-year period
▸ Over four months, led a team of six people to digitize 2,000 financial documents and create a more streamlined fundraising process

NON PROFIT B ▪ Milwaukee, WI ▪ June 2011–October 2012
Development Associate

▸ Coordinated fundraising efforts to build playgrounds in low-income areas
▸ Managed event coordination for the inaugural "Come Play, Milwaukee," a 500+ person cocktail party and fundraiser that exceeded expectations and brought in $350,000; oversaw caterer, decorations, sponsorships, live music and silent auction
▸ Wrote organization's weekly blog posts, grew email list from 110 to 1,200 people and created tracking spreadsheets to better organize fundraising efforts

AFFILIATIONS

▸ Member, Big Trade Association (DC Chapter)
▸ Member, Big Digital Association (DC Chapter)

EDUCATION

B.A. in philosophy, Big State University
Graduated 2011

The Explanation

You might think, "This resume doesn't feel very long." And you would be right.

Here's the deal with resumes: you don't earn extra credit when you include a ton of information. In fact, I believe a wordy resume that spills onto two or three pages hurts you. That's because employers either don't read the entire document or can't discern the most important parts.

With resumes, it's not about including everything. It's about including the RIGHT things.

Here's a section-by-section breakdown.

Bio Information

Standard stuff with your name, email, phone and address. The two wrinkles are your LinkedIn profile and a new idea called a "personal hashtag." With a personal hashtag, you can share your best stuff on Twitter like an online resume.

See page 165 for help with your LinkedIn profile summary and page 50 for more on a personal hashtag campaign.

Introductory Lines

Give the employer two sentences on your career to this point. That's plenty. Rely on numbers (ex: $2.4 million) and details (ex: three capital campaigns) rather than empty jargon like "motivated" as we discuss on page 207.

Skills

In the Skills section, it's all about practical, technical abilities. Stay away from "skills" like "excellent time management." That's important, sure, but on a resume, the employer needs to know what you can do in the job.

That's why Joseph Green, who wants a new position in development/fundraising, makes clear he has strong command of fundraising and e-marketing tools. Now the employer knows he can handle, for instance, fundraising campaigns on popular crowdfunding sites. That information is more valuable than if he claims he's a "fast worker."

Experience

Brevity and details are key. Note how, in the first bullet, Joseph explains the nature of the work at each organization but doesn't dwell on it too long.

Part of a team that raises more than $8 million annually for cancer research.

Cancer research, $8 million. Got it. Moving on.

Then, he offers two bullet points that focus on hard numbers and his ability to turn challenges into opportunities.

Over four months, led a team of six people to digitize over 2,000 financial documents and create a more streamlined fundraising process.

Managed event coordination for the inaugural "Come Play, Milwaukee," a 500+ person cocktail party and fundraiser that exceeded expectations and brought in $350,000.

The hard numbers:

- Four months
- Team of six
- 2,000 financial documents
- 500+ person cocktail party and fundraiser
- $350,000

Problem solving:

- Transformed the organization from paper to digital and helped it become more competitive for fundraising dollars
- Took a brand-new concept for a cocktail party and made it a success in year one

Affiliations

Joseph is a member of two organizations relevant to the job and his industry. So he lists them. He also makes sure to spell out any abbreviations and doesn't assume the reader knows what they mean (Big Trade Association and not "BTA").

Education

Education goes at the bottom of a resume. Your skills and work experience matter more than where you went to college.

Education at the bottom applies even if it's a super-impressive school, and you had a 4.0 GPA.

How to keep your resume to one page

In the last section, I explain why you need a one-page resume. Still, you might have a lengthy work history and think, "How am I supposed to put all of my jobs on *one page?*"

The key to a one-pager is to limit the number of bullet points below each job. The latest job receives the most description, but after that keep the bullet points to a minimum. It saves space and also helps the employer focus on your biggest achievement(s). Less is more.

Let's use the resume template from pages 211–215 as a guide and imagine the person has held four jobs instead of two. How do we describe all four but keep the resume to one page?

EXPERIENCE

COMPANY NAME * City, State * Start Date–End Date

Job Title

- ▸ Explain the company and its general purpose
- ▸ Work accomplishment #1
- ▸ Work accomplishment #2
- ▸ Work accomplishment #3

COMPANY NAME * City, State * Start Date–End Date

Job Title

- ▸ Explain the company and its general purpose
- ▸ Work accomplishment #1
- ▸ Work accomplishment #2

COMPANY NAME * City, State * Start Date–End Date
Job Title
- ▸ Explain the company and its general purpose
- ▸ Work accomplishment #1
- ▸ (Work accomplishment #2 if space allows)

COMPANY NAME * City, State * Start Date–End Date
Job Title
- ▸ Explain the company and its general purpose
- ▸ Work accomplishment #1
- ▸ (Work accomplishment #2 if space allows)

Explanation

Notice how I give three work accomplishments for the latest job. Then, I provide two examples for job #2 and one each for jobs #3 and #4. That's all the space I likely have.

Each time, I include the bullet that explains the company (examples on page 212), which helps the employer understand the nature of the work. If you don't have room for the "explanation" bullet point, then let it go. But do your best to keep it in there; context is critical.

Remember to rely on numbers/stats in each "accomplishment" and explain how you overcame challenges to solve problems. Each bullet should be no longer than two lines.

Finally, if you can't keep the resume to one page, consider widening the margins *slightly* to –.3" to the left and –.3" to the right. In Microsoft Word, it's found in the "Paragraph" settings under the "Indentation" options. Don't take the margins too wide — it will make your resume look odd and could distract the employer.

Please don't use those little black dots

More and more, I see people "rank" their talents on resumes, and it's a plain dumb idea. Ever seen one of these?

SKILLS

Social media	●	●	●	●	●
Public speaking	●	●	●	○	○
Marketing	●	●	●	●	●
Writing	●	●	●	●	●
Leadership	●	●	●	●	○

Why do I loath these black and white dots? Let me count the ways.

1. Don't judge your own skills

As you apply for jobs, let employers assess your ability. The person in the above example claims to have "five dot" writing ability, but maybe a boss is a much better writer and thinks, "Five dots? I don't think so."

You provide the goods (writing samples), and employers (panel of judges) will give you a score. Don't rank yourself.

2. The dots say nothing about you

In the example above, the person grants himself "Five dot" status for social media. What is the employer supposed to think? "Oh wow, five dots! He must know EVERYTHING about social media. Quick! Someone call this guy before Mark Zuckerberg snatches him away!"

The little black dots mean little and if you do have solid SM experience, then the dots works against you.

What if you know how to manage Facebook pages, advertise on Twitter, lead groups on LinkedIn and build Pinterest boards? That's great experience, but you wipe it all away with five measly circles.

Explain to employers (and robotic scanners looking for keywords) the depth of your skills. Ditch the dots.

3. You choose style over substance

I don't care how sleek and stylish it looks to add a row of black dots. Your actual experience is more beautiful than any graphic design.

Employers need to see what you can physically do on the job. Showcase your ability, step back and let the judges hand you a score.

You might be a "Perfect 10" after all, but it's not for you to decide.

How to account for resume gaps

What if you have a "gap" in your resume, a period of time in which extenuating circumstances kept you from the workforce (ex: serious injury, illness or care for a family member).

The employer who scans your resume might think, "Why does she have a two-year gap in work history? What happened during that time?"

The most appropriate way to explain to the "gap," in my view, is a note at the bottom of your "experience" section.

I don't advocate a note about a "gap" if you spent several months looking for work. The advice here only applies to circumstances beyond your control.

Let's use the resume template from page 211 but change the dates to reflect a gap.

EXPERIENCE

NON PROFIT A ▪ Washington, DC ▪ November 2012– Present

Associate Director of Development

- ▶ Part of an organization that raises more than $8 million annually for cancer research
- ▶ Grew organization's social media presence 400% over two-year period
- ▶ Over four months, led a team of six people to digitize 2,000 financial documents and create a more streamlined fundraising process

NON PROFIT B ▪ Milwaukee, WI ▪ June 2010–October 2011

Development Associate

- ▶ Coordinated fundraising efforts to build playgrounds in low-income areas
- ▶ Managed event coordination for the inaugural "Come Play, Milwaukee," a cocktail party and fundraiser that exceeded expectations and brought in $350,000; oversaw caterer, decorations, sponsorships, live music and silent auction
- ▶ Wrote organization's weekly blog posts, grew email list from 110 to 1,200 people and created tracking spreadsheets to better organize fundraising efforts

*Note: Spent November 2011–October 2012 caring for an ailing relative and returned to the workforce in November 2012.

A short explanation at the bottom of your work history is all you need. Don't go into great detail or provide a full paragraph.

Again, do not write a line like "*Note: Spent 2013 jobhunting." The "gap" explanation applies if you physically could not work due to an unforeseen or unpreventable situation.

Chapter 11
List Posts with a Purpose

The Lists

4 QUESTIONS EVERYONE SHOULD ASK IN A JOB INTERVIEW

Every part of the hiring process counts, but a face-to-face meeting is the best opportunity to dazzle the boss and land a coveted offer.

To maximize those precious moments, here are the four types of interview questions everyone should ask an employer.

Each question demonstrates critical thinking and declares: I'm in it to win it.

Scenario: you interview to do marketing/communications for a grocery chain.

1. The Background Check

People love to talk about themselves. Period. If you come prepared with a question about the boss's career (thanks to LinkedIn or a website bio), he will perk up, brag on himself and find you impressive — even though you only asked a question and listened.

Sample interview question

"I noticed you started your career in marketing for Ringling Brothers circus. What was that experience like?"

2. The Office Insight

Every company has a website. So read it before the interview. Check out past and current projects, staff bios and gain a general sense of the office culture. Then, drop a question to prove you did your homework.

Sample interview question

"I read several of your recent press releases and saw you're making a push to carry more gluten-free products. How big is the demand right now for gluten-free foods?"

3. The "Wow" Factor

The bio question, the company question…both solid. Now, turn your focus to the industry, in general. Read news about the grocery biz and put the company in context with the latest headlines. That's next-level stuff, which prompts a "wow" from the boss.

Sample interview question

"I see Acme Corporation bought Little Corporation. The deal seems like a major shake-up in the grocery industry. What does the Acme Corporation takeover say to you?"

4. The Inception

With the "wow" question, you took the interview from an uncomfortable boss-applicant arrangement to a conversation among peers. Now, plant a seed in the manager's brain with a cool marketing idea. Make him feel like he needs you on the team right now.

Sample interview question

"I like the way your store offers online deals based on my previous purchases. For me, a twentysomething, it's a smart strategy. Wouldn't it be cool to do a targeted campaign to reach people where they spend time online?"

Boss says, "You know, that's a really good idea."

———

For your next job interview, come with a set of questions no one else will have.

Be smarter. Be one notch better.

Be different.

9 reasons every 20-something needs a side hustle

Have a few extra minutes each week? I know you do. We all do.

Skip the trendy new TV show everyone talks about. Look away from social media.

Pick a side hustle and build on it over time.

Here are nine good reasons.

1. You'll learn all kinds of stuff you might not at your actual job

Too often, our day jobs become routine or fail to challenge us. Find a side hustle that inspires, and you will grow by leaps and bounds. Why? Because it will be something you want for yourself.

2. A side hustle could lead to a new career

Rather than quit your job and move to something new, dabble on the side. Test the waters, see if there's potential (ahem, money) and if the opportunity shows promise, then make your move.

3. Your twenties are the best years to hustle

As twentysomethings, many of us are single or without kids. With a flexible schedule, it's the perfect decade to experiment with projects we're passionate about and find where we belong. Bust it in your twenties, and the hard work will pave the way for a life of purpose.

4. You will become a time management champion

With a full-time job and side hustle, you begin to look at 24 hours strategically. Now you find spare minutes before work or squeeze in a few before bed. If you're chasing a dream, time management keeps you on track and on the grind.

5. Your twenties are all about taking chances

Nothing ventured, nothing gained. So your side hustle fails. OK, move on and try another. Some of the biggest life lessons happen when things don't work out. Roll the dice because even when you lose, you win.

6. Your side hustle will make you better at your real job

Never forget: all skills are transferable. You might pick up a cool design strategy while you create an app. Those skills could then inform your judgment at your day job. One hand feeds the other, and no time is wasted — even if your side hustle doesn't pay.

7. You will keep your mind active

If you put your brain on "shutdown mode" the minute work ends, you leave all kinds of productivity on the table. A side hustle makes you more inquisitive and more capable. Like playing a sport or an instrument, the more you train your mind, the sharper it becomes.

8. You might stumble into your true passion

If you like music, find a way to spend time in that space. If you like to write, start a blog or contribute to one. Spend time with people and places you enjoy, and you could fall into a role that is fulfilling. Without a side hustle, you may never find it.

9. You're worth more than a 9-to-5

A full-time job, even one that requires a 60-hour schedule, won't teach us everything. And too often we're more concerned about the company's bottom line than our own.

Each week, build in time to do what you love. The results will surprise you.

10 reasons every 20-something should spend time in a big city

Yes, big cities are expensive, noisy and crowded. They can also make you stronger and more successful in your career.

Here are ten reasons why.

1. Big cities make you grow up quickly

One week in a "big city" and you realize people are less compassionate about your issues and more concerned with their own. It's not the cozy, safe college campus you once knew.

Big cities have an edge to them. Only the tough among us win out.

2. Big cities put you in another gear

The minute you walk out the door each morning, you go. You blow past the crowds to make the bus before the door closes, scurry across an intersection to avoid a wave of oncoming traffic and hustle in the office because, well, everyone else moves fast too.

The ability to work quickly will then follow you the rest of your career.

3. You deal with massive egos

Where do "important" people work? At the top of skyscrapers in big cities, that's where.

One day, you'll look back and laugh. One day, you'll realize how "that crazy boss" made you disciplined enough to handle anyone.

4. You say hello to the world

Big cities are full of opportunity so twentysomethings from seemingly every country descend on them. Soon enough, you befriend people from all walks of life (foreign and American), broaden your worldview and begin to understand where you fit.

5. You learn to budget your money

Everything costs more in a metro area. Rent, food, clothes. It's humbling to say, "Don't think I can go out tonight. Need to save a little."

No, you can't pay the bills with a reality check, but it's worth a hell of a lot. And being frugal in your 20s will keep your credit score high and debt low.

6. You get knocked down

Some jerk at the office will tear you apart when you make a mistake. Some crazy landlord will scream at you for loud music (even though it wasn't). Some hotshot businessman will actually knock you to the ground as he runs to catch the subway — while on his phone — at 6:07 p.m.

That's OK. I hope you pick up a few bumps and bruises. You'll heal and be better for it.

7. Huge ideas happen in a crowded place

Young professionals move to big cities because they want the action. They thrive on it. And if you add enough young people into an urban center, pretty soon they'll come together and create brilliant new ideas. You gotta be in the mix too.

8. Big cities make you live with less

Smaller apartment = less furniture. Smaller bedroom = less mattress. Smaller closet = less clothes.

In a big city, you learn to sacrifice. In exchange, you receive the perks of a metropolis: a wealth of culture, food, entertainment and a fervent energy that breathes life into everything — even at 11 p.m. on a random Wednesday night.

9. Never a dull moment

Always a cool concert. Always a huge festival. Always a new restaurant you HAVE TO try.

You're never bored in a big city or allowed to say, "There's nothing to do." That's reserved for people in the suburbs.

10. Big cities set you up for success

After time in the big city, no challenge is too daunting, no person too demanding and no moment too intimidating.

You emerge from the chaos stronger and sharper.

17 things you are 100% capable of doing right now

Mind over matter. That's all it is.

Here's what I mean:

1. You can take steps to better your career whenever you want. There are no rules, and there are no limits. You can get started right now.

2. You can teach yourself something new and become instantly more valuable. Yes, you.

3. You can send an email to your best buds and set in motion the cool app you always talk about building together.

4. You can give a co-worker a compliment and make her day.

5. You can start a blog and use it to take your career to an entirely different level.

6. You can knock out the one task you've been meaning to do for a while. And then it's done.

7. You can download a classic book on leadership or new-age book on business and start reading it during your lunch break.

8. You can make stuff happen *for* you rather than wait for stuff to happen *to* you.

9. You can email someone you respect and schedule a time for coffee to listen and absorb his/her wisdom. Yep, you can do that right now.

10. You can fight through a challenge rather than give up because the solution didn't come easily. I know you can.

11. You can decide to take that hobby of yours more seriously. Oh, the many merits of a side hustle.

12. You can go online, find a networking event and make plans to attend. And once you're there, you can walk up to anyone and begin a conversation. Why? Because you are 100 percent capable.

13. You can go above and beyond right now even though no one asked you to.

14. You can fire off a thank-you email to someone who helped you out recently. You can certainly find 60 seconds to do it.

15. You can produce your best work today. What's stopping you?

16. You can hop up from your desk and ask a colleague you respect, "Hey, can you show me how to do that?"

17. You can go as far as you want today. All from your seat. Nothing holding you back.

The day is yours. Go get it!

25 things every young professional should know by age 25 (search this list post on Amazon for the full ebook)

Before you hit the big two–five, you should know the following list backwards and forwards.

25. The word is spelled "definitely," not "definately."

24. Read an apartment lease before you sign. ALL of it.

23. An Excel PivotTable will change your life.

22. A cover letter should add color and personality. It shouldn't summarize your resume.

21. Everyone likes to receive praise, but the smartest young adults seek constructive criticism.

20. The days of a college syllabus are long gone. If you're waiting for someone to give you direction, have a seat. You'll be there a while.

19. Multi-tasking is great, but some moments require your undivided attention.

18. Take LinkedIn seriously.

17. Understand the pay-stub that accompanies your paycheck.

16. There's no such thing as an overnight success. However, people who do "break through" tend to start their day while others are still asleep.

15. Know the difference between a Roth IRA and Traditional IRA.

14. Even though college is over, you should still find extracurriculars. Among the many reasons, clubs and organizations are terrific places to network.

13. You're never too busy to write a thank-you note.

12. Negotiate your salary.

11. The ability to follow-through on assignments can take you from 25-year-old newbie to essential team member.

10. You probably make more money than some of your friends and less than others. The only thing that matters is that you pay your own bills on time.

9. Bring a lunch to work. It's healthier and cheaper than eating out.

8. Don't step into an interview room without research on the company and smart questions for the employer.

7. Dropbox. Learn it and love it.

6. Treat interns with respect. They'll provide you with management training and ease your workload.

5. To impress older business associates, ask about their own career path. You may also learn a thing or two.

4. Under-promise. Over-deliver.

3. The less you write, the tighter the message. The less you talk, the stronger the speech.

2. The only failure in your 20s is inaction. Everything else is trial and error.

1. You're halfway through the most formative decade of your life. You don't need all the answers, but you must keep asking questions. Start with this one: what's something new I can learn right now?

101 skills I learned after two years of blogging

From WordPress to Google Analytics to legal stuff like forming an LLC, News To Live By, my blog, has become a real-world master's degree.

Why should you start a blog?

- ▸ To cultivate a topic or issue you're passionate about
- ▸ To create a portfolio that will enhance your resume and job search
- ▸ To become smarter and more capable at the job you already have

The harder you work on yourself, the more opportunity comes your way.

WordPress (blog platform) taught me how to...

1. Create a website from scratch (the first step is always the hardest)

2. Pick a domain and hosting provider

3. Write and publish articles

4. Organize and categorize my work

5. Use various plugins to customize the site

6. Optimize articles for search engines

7. Tag articles with relevant keywords

8. Do (basic) alterations to the site code

9. Use links to make the content more interesting

10. Be entrepreneurial, roll the dice and make my own luck

MailChimp (e-newsletter platform) taught me how to...

11. Create an e-newsletter

12. Grow an e-newsletter subscriber list

13. Use data analytics to fine-tune my email campaigns

14. Tailor an e-newsletter for viewing on mobile devices

15. Write strong email subject lines

My ebook, *25 Things Every Young Professional Should Know by Age 25,* taught me how to...

16. Stay disciplined enough to finish writing it

17. Design a snazzy cover so people notice it

18. Use an ebook book to encourage email subscribers

19. Publish and sell through Amazon (easier than I thought it would be)

20. Market myself in person

Google Analytics taught me how to...

21. Understand how traffic flows into (and out of) a website

22. Tweak my content based on what people like to read most

23. Research the organic keywords people use to find my site

24. See the links people click and the ones they don't

25. Live with the fact that, when I started, I had roughly five views a day (mostly from my wife)

The daily grind of blogging taught me how to...

26. Stay committed to the project no matter what

27. Ensure every blog post has meaning and relevance

28. Stick to self-imposed deadlines

29. Always try to outdo myself with the next article

30. Be patient and enjoy watching something grow little by little

31. Push past the days when I think, "What the hell am I doing with all this blogging?"

32. Find a way through a challenge even if it's totally foreign to me

33. Accept that I will make mistakes...

34. ...and be observant enough to fix them

35. Realize if I'm passionate about the work, it's not actually work

All the tweeting taught me how to...

36. Use @DannyHRubin as a powerful networking tool on Twitter

37. Learn the Twitter "lingo" and keep up with savvy users

38. Understand what it means to "DM" someone

39. Use Tweepi to clean up my list and keep it growing

40. Stick with Twitter long enough to "get" why it's so great

My Facebook fan page taught me how to...

41. Treat the fan page differently than my profile page

42. Understand the "Insights" section and use the data to strengthen my content

43. Create fun memes

44. Appreciate the 1,000-fan milestone (not easy to reach)

45. Focus on quality over quantity

The legal stuff taught me how to...

46. Register a trademark with the US Patent and Trademark Office (took almost a year)

47. Create an LLC and incorporate the blog (Woo-hoo! I'm a small business owner!)

48. Write an FTC disclosure statement

49. Obtain fair-use photos and give proper attribution

50. Legally protect myself and my investment (the blog) at every turn

My blogging niche (millennials and careers) taught me how to...

51. Develop and nurture relationships with other people in the Gen Y career space

52. Focus on one topic instead of trying to be all things to all people

53. Offer advice that's hands-on and useful

54. Highlight the great work of others as often as I can

55. Listen to the audience and deliver answers people need

All the writing taught me how to...

56. Find my voice

57. Become a shrewd editor

58. Talk "with" the reader and not "at" the reader

59. Make my articles move quickly so you don't become bored

60. Cut out useless words like "in order" and "that"

61. Write list posts people want to share

62. Take negative commenters in stride

63. Set aside my feelings and use criticism to improve

64. Say a lot with a little

65. Become a more effective communicator (the most important job skill a young adult can have)

The busy work to maintain the blog taught me how to...

66. Rely on Hootsuite to schedule content ahead of time

67. Use TweetDeck to monitor various Twitter feeds at once

68. Take advantage of Click to Tweet to make quotable lines easy to share

69. Tap into Help a Reporter Out (HARO) to find interview subjects

70. Use Google to answer all sorts of questions

Online advertising taught me how to...

71. Dabble with affiliate marketing

72. Only promote or endorse a product I genuinely believe in

73. Not clutter a site with ads. If I don't like tons of ads, why would you?

Being a newbie at blogging taught me how to...

74. Follow SEOMoz to learn how the internet works

75. Seek people with knowledge about websites and how to build an audience

76. Read news columnists I respect and learn from them

77. Try to figure out a problem and, if I'm truly stuck, ask someone I respect

78. Choose Wordpress.org over WordPress.com

79. Build an email subscriber list (took me seven months to figure that out)

80. Keep it simple, stupid

Other skills and tools I picked up the past two years...

81. Writing and editing tips from Copyblogger

82. Encourage email signups with LeadPages

83. Use Pinterest thanks to frequent posting on #MillennialScoop (I'm a guy... give me a break on coming late to Pinterest)

84. The ability to create a (decent enough) infographic

85. How to send mail-merge emails

86. Research keywords and phrases with Google AdWords

87. Manage an ad with Google AdSense

88. De-bug a link so it displays properly on Facebook

89. Set up a PayPal business account and use it to accept payments

90. Embed video into an e-newsletter campaign

91. Record "how-to" career videos and use them to deliver value back to the audience

92. Be part of a live webinar on career advice

93. Learn the power of a handwritten note (writing and receiving)

94. Wrap my head around Google+

95. Create a survey with Google Forms and Survey Monkey

The biggest takeaways from two years of blogging...

96. There is no deadline or end-goal. I learn as I go and work on the website as best I can. What ultimately happens with News To Live By will be a direct result of how much effort I put in. Simple as that.

97. Everything about a blog is a slow grind, but the longer I hang around the more valuable it becomes.

98. I must give before I can get. Every. Single. Time.

99. A blog is a tremendous marketing tool. It's much easier to show people what I can do rather than tell them.

100. News To Live By has allowed me to pursue my passion. And that's so cool; to have a blank canvas to do what I love. What's better than that?

101. In years three, four and beyond, I have a lot more to learn.

———

One blog. 101 skills.

Imagine what you can learn from your OWN website.

Conclusion

WELCOME TO THE END. BY NOW, I HOPE YOU REALIZE *WAIT, HOW DO I WRITE THIS EMAIL?* IS NOT A SERIES OF EDITING AND GRAMMAR LESSONS. RATHER, THE BOOK IS A GUIDE ON HOW TO MAKE A LASTING IMPRESSION WITH THE WRITTEN WORD.

We often hear people talk about the importance of "hard" and "soft" skills. By "hard" skills, I mean software and tools you know how to use. "Soft" skills are more like networking and building relationships.

Effective writing also contains "hard" and "soft" skills. The former is the use of strong detail as we describe our work experience. The latter is how we employ our words to engage in meaningful conversation.

As you craft emails and documents, I want you to now think with both sides of your brain, so to speak. Write in specifics ("hard" skills) and with a curiosity for others ("soft" skills).

Effective writing opens doors, fosters relationships and cements your value. With the book as your guide, every email and document will read well, help you build trust and set you apart.

An email inbox is a crowded place.

Make every word count.

Thank You

WAIT, HOW DO I WRITE THIS EMAIL? IS THE CULMINATION OF EVERY COMMUNICATION SKILL I HAVE LEARNED SO FAR. THAT MEANS I NEED TO THANK PEOPLE WHO TAUGHT, MENTORED AND SUPPORTED ME WELL BEFORE I EVER HAD A BLOG OR THE DESIRE TO WRITE A BOOK. WITHOUT THEM, THERE WOULD BE NO BOOK.

First, the ultimate thanks to my wife, Shikma. You're my best friend, sounding board and the person who most understands the journey from personal blog to book. When I need your advice, you're right there. When I need your feedback, you're patient and exact. And you brought me back to earth when I asked, "Why the hell am I writing a book? Is this even a good idea?" Thank you for everything.

To my parents, Joel and Sara Jo, who recognized my early love of writing and made sure I had opportunities to hone the skill. I think back to when I was ten and you asked the editor of a community newsletter if I could write a review of *Major League II*. (Roger Ebert had nothing on me.)

Thank you Mom for your belief that somehow, some way I would do something meaningful with all this writing. And thank you Dad for editing my work as far back as the *Major League II* review. How many kids have their writing edited for grammar and style before they enter middle school? I used to hate the criticism; now, I consider it a blessing.

And a giant thanks to my sister, Molly, who has not only supported my writing but also made a huge impact on the book. Thank you for your honesty and critiques as the project came together. I'm grateful to have you in my corner then, now and always.

As for my career, thank you to Shane Moreland, my first television news director, who took a chance on a rookie reporter and gave me my first job. To Jack McKenzie and Rob Yarin at my second job, media consulting company Frank N. Magid Associates, for your willingness to teach me the business side of journalism. In that time, I developed the idea for News To Live By, which shows millennials the career advice in the headlines.

There are so many people who impacted (and continue to impact) News To Live By, the blog from which I created *Wait, How Do I Write This Email?*. Whether you provided a quick favor, small tip or constant guidance, I owe you a lot. I preach the value of a side hustle (my blog) because it's important to learn new skills and do the work we love. I didn't expect to form so many relationships through the experience. I'm thankful for Ryan Sullivan (wpsitecare.com), Chelsea Krost (chelseakrost.com), Paul Angone (allgroanup.com), Jon Mertz (thindifference.com), Amanda Augustine (jobsearchamanda.com), Jenna Goudreau (businessinsider.com), Joe and John McCormack (thebrieflab.com) and Ron Culp (culpwrit.com).

When I decided to write a book, I felt like I stared up the face of a mountain. I had 1,000 questions and few answers. Fortunately, I received guidance from a collection of publishing professionals and critical feedback from friends and family. Thank you to Karen Jones (kjwriter.com), who taught me how to construct a solid book proposal and spent considerable time editing and refining the book's idea. It's rare to find someone so willing to help…just because. Even though I decided to independently publish, the proposal phase forced me to think hard about the book and what it should contain. It was time well spent. I also owe a big thanks to Scott Spiewak (freshimpactpr.com) for your insight into the publishing process and the best ways to make the book a reality. You know how "the game" is played, and I appreciate your candor.

Thanks to Debra Englander, who edited the book and took an immediate interest in the "email template" idea. As a blogger, I have to be my own editor, and it was a luxury to have you over my shoulder fine tuning each page.

A big thanks to Paul McCarthy (paulmccarthydesign.com) for his expert design work on the front cover and to 1106 Design (1106design.com) for the book's interior. Thank you, Michele DeFilippo and Ronda Rawlins, for making the process collaborative and dealing with my many tweaks and questions. I'm glad I put the book in the hands of professionals and didn't try to do it myself.

Finally, to all my friends and family members, thank you for recommendations on chapters to include (and remove) and your general impressions on how you would use the book in your lives. I trust each of you 100 percent and rely on your perspective. Thanks for always having time for me.

As I hold *Wait, How Do I Write This Email?* in my hands, it feels like a trip through my life from the *Major League II* review to the hours and hours I spent writing, editing and designing the finished product. The book is the next chapter in my professional journey, and I hope it plays an important role in yours too.

When you arrive at the work you're meant to do, remember the people who lit the path and showed you the way.

After all, they led you to your true purpose.

I think that's worth a thank you.

Index